Gathering The Fragments That Nothing Will Be Lost

YAH-*Scribe*
PUBLISHING

First Printing: 2020

Paperback ISBN: 978-1-7923-5103-7

E-Book ISBN:

YAH-Scribe Publishing, LLC
24901 Northwestern Hwy Frontage Rd #220
Southfield, MI 48075
www.yahscribe.com

CONTENTS

Foreword

Luke 22:31-32 King James Version (KJV)
And the Lord said, Simon, Simon, behold, Satan hath desired to have you, that he may sift you as wheat: [32] But I have prayed for thee, that thy faith fail not: and when thou art converted, strengthen thy brethren.

Author and Prophet Linda Hunt, has done it again! Much like her, masterful literary work in "Amen Sister', in these pages, of her latest work, "Gathering the Fragments That Nothing Will Be Lost," we find poignant truths. Truths that will cause the reader to shutter as they consider the endurance of each Woman's Cross, beginning with Prophet Linda's. Yet, through their Faithfulness to a Faithful God, they each have earned their Crown of Restoration, Honor, and Recognition!

In an hour where God is Highlighting, Women, and in particular, His Daughters. His Servant Leader, Prophet Linda Hunt, is one that has been behind the Mountains and in the Shadows for many years, in many respects. But God, Himself is Orchestrating her Grand & Greater Debut! As a Servant Leader, it would be uncharacteristic of, Prophet Linda, if she didn't go back and Gather the Spoils, born out of the Fragments of the lives of the other women whose stories are featured here in this, Anthology!

As I read, Gathering the Fragments, I experienced a range of emotions, that drew me in as a woman, a servant, a covenant sister, as a human being, a wife, a minister, and as a Prophet of God! In reading, Prophet Linda's testimony, I have gained much insight! I now realize why she has such a deep passion for seeing women and men live out their God Given Destiny! I understand why the depths of frustration when she encounters potential that is seeming, in her experience, locked up and locked down! My appreciation for the grace and gift upon her life, to push, provoke, and promote others, amplifying her witness, as a Marketplace Connector, has increased dramatically!

Although I have known, loved, and respected this great, Woman of God, for many years in no way, had I fully understood, nor appreciated the price she has paid through the pain, long-suffering, and public humiliation for the anointing, upon her life. As a Servant Leader, Published Author, Marketplace Minister, and Prophet of God!

I am humbled by her transparency evidenced in these pages. This is further proof that Prophet Linda is committed to carrying out the work whereto she has been called, exemplifying courage, humility, love, and obedience necessary for the fulfillment of the Charge!

Showcased in these stories, are women, who in many respects, are diverse, in their depiction, degradation, and depths of the suffering experienced, yet, share the commonality of public pain! Through their, Test and Trails, including but not limited to: Abuse, Adoption, Church Hurt, Divorce, Homosexuality, Neglect, resulting in trauma for some, nevertheless, their testimony reveals, there is a, "Balm in Gilead"! As you will read, only through prayer, the word of God, (Ps 107:20), support, wise counsel, patience, persistence, perseverance, and deliverance, have they been sustained, and have prevailed! In their debut, these overcomers are privileged to share their journey with the

World. All to and for the Glory of God!

As we eagerly await the conclusion of the matter, in the Fall of 2020. Our prayer is that each and every person who reads these transformational testimonies, whether you feel as though you have been, Sifted as Wheat, or Beautifully Broken, "Gathering of the Fragments," will be instrumental in you being strengthened and converted! After you have strengthened and converted, you, too, will be among those that are charged to go back and strengthen and convert others!

It is my distinct honor to have been afforded the privilege to write this forward on behalf of God's Servant Leader and Prophet, Linda Hunt!

Prophet, Dr. Beverly Jordan
Dr. Beverly Jordan Global Ministries
Detroit, MI

Introduction

Connecting with amazing women is something I look forward to doing regularly on this journey. That expectation was no different when I met Ms. Linda Hunt. I quickly recognized her great desire to help women overcome hindering obstacles in life because it is near and dear to my heart as well. After being interviewed on her radio show I knew there were more ways for us to impact women across the globe. What better way than through our common love... sharing the testimonies of our lives and helping others do the same. I am humbled to jump start your journey of gathering the **Fragments** of your life because **NOTHING'S** lost!

When you hear the word "fragments" the first thing you may think about, more than likely than not, is broken pieces of something. Maybe broken glass, breadcrumbs, or even shattered dreams. For the most part, your thoughts are correct. But the important factor is that you never discard the fragments.

Life experiences may have you believing that you sometimes get the short end of the stick but that short end can still be used. You have the choice to allow God to take the fragments of your life and create something glorious. It may NOT look or feel good in the process but, in the end, nothing shall be lost and that includes the fragments.

As you embark on this journey, to overcome the fragmentation of your life through the pages of this book, it is imperative for you to allow God to mold and shape you into the magnificent being that you were created to be. One thing I know to be true is - God doesn't miss anything. Everything you have gone through and everything you will go through will be used to enhance your experience of life.

The Breaking

The creation process began with breaking... God spoke to break the world from darkness, He spoke to break the heavens from the earth, the water from land, and so on. The breaking process is required so that whatever is being created can start in its purest form. See, you may have thought that your life experiences were created to break you in a negative sense but if you look at the growth process you will find that in order to get a useful product something has to be broken.

For example, when a seed is put into the soil and covered up the shell of the seed breaks open, and while under the soil it begins to connect with the nutrients in the soil so a new life is created that's when the flower, plant, or vegetable begins to grow and you see life beginning to expand in a more elaborate way. You'll see the buds come up, you'll see the leaves pop out of the stem, you'll see the colors form and then you have the beautiful flower and it is the same process with you. There has been some breaking in you through childhood, adulthood, or maybe in your current reality. Either way… that was required for you to get from there to here. The question is what nutrients do you need to connect with for your new life to be created?

The Gathering

Gathering the fragments of your life is a very painful part of the process. It requires you to backtrack, relive, and release some things that you may have been holding for years. You may have even become comfortable with it but it's now time to release it. How do I know? Because you are reading this book. The Gathering is what takes time. It is the inside work that most people do not want to do. You don't really want to focus on the internal aspects of you and as such you tend to mask the outer facets of your life to appear to be whole. However, when you begin to gather the fragments of your life, from the trials, tribulations, setbacks, and disappointments you will begin to identify what is no longer serving you. You will be amazed that in the midst of the gathering process you will also see how some of the pieces can (and will) come together to be used to bless someone else which is exactly what the co-authors of this book have done.

You will read stories that will allow you to see the depths of their soul and at the very same time, you will see the depths of yours. I encourage you to move through the process with intentionality. Allow yourself to be open to a new way of acknowledging and releasing the old so you can live in the new. The overall theme of *Gathering the Fragments* is for you to understand that you are not alone, it is for you to understand that your voice matters, it is for you to understand that no matter what life has given you or allowed to happen to you it does not mean that there is no value in your fragments. So, as you begin to see yourself in these stories and reflect on what it is true for you, ask yourself, how can this bless someone else. That one step will help alleviate the pain in the process. It is your time to release the excuses and give yourself permission to be molded into wholeness.

The Molding

Clay is hard and must get wet in order to get molded. It has to be spun around on a wheel many times while having water added and little by little it begins to form into what the potter desires it to be. God is the Potter, and you are the clay!

You were broken into fragments that you will now gather so they can be used to shape you and He will do it with loving hands. Gone is the time when you could freely sit in dysfunction and chaos. Gone is the time you welcomed pity while living on *Woe Is Me Avenue*. The time has come for you to be open to accepting His unconditional gifts of abundance, acceptance, and love. He wants to shower you with His gentle caress in this season. He wants to prove to you that every blessing He promised in His word is true for you too, but <u>YOU MUST LET IT</u> GO to receive all of what He has for you. The Question is...

ARE YOU READY?

Endorsements

With so much the enemy has done to bring brokenness in the lives of so many people, especially women who have experienced so much trauma and abuse, I am excited to recommend this book called, "Gathering the Fragments Anthology". It is good to know that what Satan meant for evil, God can turn around for our good. In this book sixteen female authors chronicle their stories of how they have, through the power of God, triumphed through tragedy and went from victim to victor. Through their stories, you will be encouraged to believe God that no matter what you face, no matter what the trial, you too can overcome the mountains in your life and emerge victoriously.

Apostle Dr. Kenneth D. Hogan

Living Bread Ministries Senior Pastor and Founder

Endorsements

Unlike a lot of millennial women, I've had the pleasure and honor of having matriarchs in my life to guide me so that I don't have to make the same mistakes they have. If you are like a lot of young women and you have not had a strong female role model this book will give you just that. Each story is that of a different fragment that we do not have to gather ourselves. This book exposes trauma pain and victory and can be used as a roadmap for the younger generation. We are here to learn from our elders. Reading Gathering the Fragments is like sitting at the feet of a matriarch, gathering their pearls of wisdom.

I am proud of my granny (Linda Jean) and all the ladies that joined her on this journey.

Kayla Rejoyce Byndom

Grand Daughter

Letter From The Publisher

When God first called upon me to start a publishing company, I could not have begun to foresee the dramatic impact we would make in our clients and readers lives. As a publisher we help birth people from the supernatural into their natural destiny right here on planet earth.

This was a call that I tried so hard to ignore and fought it every time that God would bring it before me but eventually I had to give in because it was not just a vision but it was part of my destiny.

Over the course of this journey together Linda and I have met and helped numerous authors see and publish their books, most of which had a special place in my heart, but nothing has captured me more than this anthology project.

As I completed the book cover and promo material for this project I wrote, in faith the following words. *"A book that will keep you going WOW WOW WOW. Across every page is an exhilarating encounter of a true story that needed to be told."* The truth I must tell is that I had not yet read a single page of the book but surely, I tell you that as I began to layout the pages of this book the words came alive.

From page to page every story griped my heart and brought me a new compassion for people's lives and the untold stories they have walked around with for decades. This book has brought me conformation once again that indeed God has called me to help people tell their stories not just for themselves but for the greater impact of people worldwide.

This is a book that I will have on my shelf in my library for the rest of my days.

Congratulations ladies on a job executed with excellence,

Prophet Blaine
CEO | YAH-Scribe Publishing, LLC

FROM REDEMPTION TO PURPOSE

Evangelist Cathy R. Hendrix

It is an extraordinary life that has not been touched by brokenness. When we are broken, we are moved from a place of stability to instability. We may even feel as if nothing is sure anymore, and that what we believed in and gave our allegiance to may never have been real at all.

When you are a woman in Spiritual leadership, your journey is not one of privacy or isolation. Instead, it has the ability to impact the lives of others who look to you for counsel and guidance. I write as a Spiritual leader who was broken by a traumatic divorce, a second divorce to be exact.

I am a devout Christian of thirty-eight years, and a minister of twenty-five years who has preached and taught The Word of God since 1995. I pastored a church with my ex-husband for 7 years, trained ministerial staff, and served on the governing boards of my affiliate churches. I have written Biblical curriculum, served as an advisor to Senior Pastors, and spoken at many conferences, workshops, and services designed for women.

The only reason my service record is mentionable is so you have a clear picture of how the Lord has used me as a mentor and role model, which will help you understand how my trauma not only touched my life but the lives of others as well. To experience one divorce was stifling enough, but having it happen a second time shattered me to my core. It broke me in ways I never thought imaginable. I was naïve. I thought if you just loved your husband enough and he did the same, there would be nothing the two of you could not overcome, no matter how difficult. It is not that this level of commitment cannot work, it absolutely can. The problem arises when both parties fail to possess the same level of commitment. That was my problem.

This chapter will not give the greatest heed to my divorce circumstances, instead, my goal is to share my journey through the redemptive process with Jesus Christ to my purpose and new life! However, it is necessary to lay a foundation for my past experience so you may glean all the golden nuggets packed into my present life and glorious future that awaits me. Yes!

Would you agree that I sound incredibly optimistic? That is because I AM. I have JOY that is constant, peace like a river, and I enjoy the benefits of being a "Kept" woman – kept by the Lord Himself.

Believe me when I tell you, it does not get any better than this! My first marriage occurred when I was twenty-one. We were married thirteen years and blessed with two beautiful daughters. We were never spiritually compatible, yet we enjoyed a fun relationship and were blessed to grow and advance in life together. However, there came a time when it became quite obvious that my husband's heart had moved on. We tried counseling, extending forgiveness, and making a new commitment to our marriage, all to no avail. I was thirty-four years old, and this was the first time in my life that I experienced a broken heart. I finally decided to exercise my Biblical option to divorce. For me, divorce was like death - the death of my marriage. I grieved sorely over the break-up of my marriage and family, and I am unable to adequately give voice to the feelings of inadequacy and low self-esteem that became my constant companions following the rejection and abandonment by my husband. I loved him deeply. There would be a three-year season as a divorcee and single mom before I married my second husband.

The second time, I married an older man who was a minister like myself. He was an excellent provider and embraced my daughters as his own. We were married for nine years, but there came a time when he began to resent me. We started a small church together and maintained it for seven years. We loved the people in our congregation, and they loved us. We were all like a little family. My husband started exhibiting jealousy over the people's response to my ministry. I would try to "dumb things down" because I did not want him to feel bad, and I tried to avoid relationship problems at all costs. As I write this, I am now ashamed that I held back on God for the sake of man. I vowed never to commit this sin again. Yes, it is a sin because the Bible says in James 4:17:

Therefore, to him, that knoweth to do good, and doeth it not, to him, it is sin.

I knew it was good for me to preach and teach the Gospel of Jesus Christ with all that was in me; yet, there were times I held back and quenched the Holy Spirit of God for the sake of "keeping the peace" (1 Thessalonians 5:19). I suppose this demonstrates the lengths we will go to in our efforts to avoid pain. That is why I did it; I just could not bear the thought of a second failed marriage for ANY reason. I equated divorce with guilt and shame, and there was no way I was doing THAT again.

Despite my efforts to control the situation, things never got better. My husband became more aloof and estranged. One day, I happened upon information about his plans to leave me. Months later, he filed for divorce. By this time, my children were adults and no longer in our home. I moved out because I could not afford our home solely on my income. My car was eventually repossessed; I was brought to financial ruin and forced to file for protection via bankruptcy. I lost my dignity, self-worth, and bore a shame that felt like a yoke of bondage that seemed to choke the life out of me.

You cannot imagine what my thoughts were like when I was alone. Here I was, a spiritual leader, mentor, counselor, Bible-Teacher, and preacher who was admired and respected by men and women alike – and broken. I was a wounded vessel with barely enough energy to get out of bed some days, and so humiliated that I did not want to face anyone at all. Seclusion was not an option because I found out God's servants do not have the luxury of furloughs just because life has happened to them. We must often continue to function, smile, and carry out our assignments in the midst of our storms.

I suppose this is one of the ways God uses brokenness as a tool. You see, the only way I could continue carrying on was by totally and completely depending on the Lord's strength to get me through. Initially, I had no strength of my own. I learned what the Apostle Paul meant in 2 Corinthians 12:9 when he said:

> *"And he said unto me, My grace is sufficient for thee: for my strength is made perfect in weakness. Most gladly, therefore, will I rather glory in my infirmities, that the power of Christ may rest upon me."*

I was in a place where I had to trust God's application of grace in my life to be enough. In my brokenness, God's strength was put on display for all to see. I knew that it was Him working through me to do what needed to be done, until I eventually came to a place where I could celebrate my own weakness because I could see God's mighty hand; and I was comforted knowing He was with me. I learned that so long as He was with me, I would be alright. My prayers started changing. I would ask for His PRESENCE because it was my lifeline. I needed HIM more than I needed any material thing or any other person. In my pit of despair, I began seeing God in a new way. My relationship with Him deepened, and this is how it happened.

Redemption Through Prayer

I remember my mother teaching my brother and me a childhood prayer that started with, "Now I lay me down to sleep..." You may know the rest of it, but my point is, I was introduced to prayer at a very young age; and although I practiced it throughout childhood and early adulthood, I later learned it is intended to be a dialogue and not a monologue. You see, I was accustomed to going to God and telling Him what I wanted Him to know and then asking Him to bless those close to me. As I got older, I learned to be less selfish and began spending more time praying for the needs of others. Then, when I came into ministry, I learned to expand my prayer life even more to include world issues, etc. However, it was while in my broken state that I learned to listen for God's voice. No more monologues where I did all the talking. I was desperate, and I needed to hear from Him. My ability to function on a given day was predicated on hearing His voice in my spirit. He would comfort me by bringing a verse to mind, reminding me that I was His and that He would never leave me. That assurance meant everything to me, and I do mean everything. My desperation taught me how to be still His presence (Psalm 46:10). I was determined not to go anywhere until I felt the peace in my soul that was my indication it was okay to go about my day. He was there.

I cannot say enough about the importance of your prayer life. It must become as natural as breathing. It is your pipeline to the Master, and it is a primary means of communication for Him. Of course, God speaks to us through His Word, but prayer is a time of solitude, where our exclusive focus is on the Lord and the intimate connection, we have with Him. It must be a priority, and it is your responsibility to zealously protect that time. If you are not careful, that time will be snatched away by the numerous distractions in your life.

Jesus is our example, and He placed great importance on communing with the Father. The Bible tells us in Mark 1:35:
"And in the morning, rising up a great while before day, he went out, and departed into a solitary place, and there prayed.

If Jesus valued prayer, so should we. The above scripture demonstrates that He made prayer His priority because He arose before daylight and found a place where He would not be disturbed. I believe the reason prayer was so important to Jesus was because He knew He was sent to the earth on assignment, and each day He went to His Father to get instructions for that day. How much more do we need to be sure we are aligned with God's will each day?

Perhaps you are at a place in your life where you lack the energy, strength, and motivation to try again. I understand that place. However, I also realize that if you have breath in your body, you are not done! There is more life to live, and you will not be adequately equipped to live the life the Lord has for you if you are not staying connected to Him to ensure you are in His will at all times.

God's will is the perfect place for a child of God. Ask God what your purpose is, if you have not already discovered it. Prayer is a perfect time to ask God about your assignment because He wants you to know! When we are walking in our purpose, we find fulfillment, focus, and the ability to handle whatever comes our way because we remain in close fellowship with our Father. Get up from the low place! You were not created for defeat, but for victory!

Redemption through Honesty
To be healed, I had to figure out my role in the failure of both marriages. My first marriage, at the age of twenty-one, was an unequally yoked union. This was sin because it was contrary to God's command, as stated in 2 Corinthians 6:14:

"Be ye not unequally yoked together with unbelievers: for what fellowship hath righteousness with unrighteousness? and what communion hath light with darkness?"

My attraction to my ex-husband took preeminence over all I knew about God's will for relationships. It wasn't long before I was pregnant, in love, and married, in that order. Although we built a nice life together materialistically, we had no substance, and infidelity was the final blow that ended our marriage after thirteen years. I learned from this experience that you must start with the right foundation, Jesus Christ. To build upon any other foundation is to build your "house" on sand. When the wind and waves of life come crashing down, they will destroy everything in its path.

My second marriage took place for the wrong reasons. Although he was a Christian, I gave more credence in his ability to provide (because I was reeling from the financial struggle of being a single mom for three years, two kids, homeowner, etc.) than to his character. Had I been paying attention I would have known he was not a suitable life partner for me. I was blinded by my need to maintain my life instead of trusting God to see me through the difficulties I was facing in His time and His way. After nine years of marriage, my second husband left me to pursue other interests.

It is not easy to be this honest with yourself. It is difficult to acknowledge your mistakes and take responsibility for them, especially when they hurt others. My children suffered because of my poor decisions. However, I cannot stress how important this step is if you intend to be healed. Proverbs 28:13 says:

"He that covereth his sins shall not prosper: but whoso confesseth and forsaketh them shall have mercy."

1 John 1:9 – *"If we confess our sins, he is faithful and just to forgive us our sins, and to cleanse us from all unrighteousness."*

Recognition of past errors and their impact on our lives will serve us well in our future endeavors. Failure to reconcile past sins increases the probability of us repeating them down the road.

It is also possible that you bear no responsibility at all in the trauma that impacted your life. Some of us have been victims of someone else's sin, or we may have lost someone we love and wondered if we should have done something differently. It is equally important that you say that out loud as well. There are cases where the injured party blames themselves for what happened. For example, in the case of rape or incest it was not your fault at all. The perpetrator was sick, you were victimized, and you do no longer have to bear the shame and guilt of that experience. God has a good plan for your life.

After these honest confessions to the Lord, I realized it was in my best interest to put relationships on hold and pursue God with everything in me. That was no easy task, and I admit that loneliness was a hard battle for me after having spent 22 years in marriage. I did entertain a suitor for a brief moment; however, it came to naught, and I knew that was for the best. I am now approaching seven years of exclusivity with God, and it has been an amazing journey.

I Changed My Mind
There came a time when I realized the trauma that broke me was not the sum total of my existence. You see, the devil has a way of messing with our heads. He magnifies our pain and failures then encourages us to rehearse it day after day until we feel completely defeated and devalued.

It is important to nourish ourselves from God's perspective of who we are. You see, we must not glorify the incident above God's ability to heal, deliver, and set us free. Jesus is THE HEALER and DELIVERER of whatever you are fighting. He offers us the opportunity to be redeemed and restored, but we must make the conscious decision to accept His offer. He will not force it on us.

It was my responsibility to change my mind. I literally had to fight for my mental health by casting down imaginations and bringing captive every thought to the obedience of Christ (2 Corinthians 10:5). It was a daily struggle, but over time it became easier and natural to resist thoughts contrary to God's Word. The mind is Satan's playground. All sin begins in the mind with a thought. If we do not arrest a sinful thought while it is a mere seed, it will grow and consume more of our thought process. Then it will infiltrate our imagination, and we will begin visualizing the reality of the sin. Then, before we know it, we are consumed and carry out the sinful act that grieves our Lord.

For God to redeem you, you must agree with Him. You must purpose in your heart and mind that the Word of God is the *truth* by which you will measure all things. For example, when Satan would tell me I was a complete failure to the Body of Christ because I was divorced, I countered that accusation with 1 Samuel 16:7(b):

"...*for the LORD seeth not as man seeth; for man looketh on the outward appearance, but the LORD looketh on the heart.*"

Nothing had changed with my heart. I loved and served God before the divorce, and I still loved and served God. God knew that, and it did not matter if anyone outside of Him saw failure. He saw a redemptive opportunity.

Rebirth
The Prophet Jeremiah tells the story of his experience at the Potter's House in Jeremiah 18. The short version is that when the clay is marred, the potter can put it back on his potter's wheel and make it over again. I think you know where I am going with this. My life was damaged, the Lord is the potter, and He alone had the power to redeem me and make me over again. However, this time He had my undivided attention, I would be totally surrendered to Him and

cooperate with His plan. This was possible because I experienced a death to SELF. I now knew what Jesus meant in Matthew 16:24:

"Then said Jesus unto his disciples, If any man will come after me, let him deny himself, and take up his cross, and follow me."

A critical step in your rebirth is forgiving those who harmed you. You may need to forgive yourself as well. Forgiveness is like power-washing your heart. If you allow God to guide you through it, you will come out brand new, baggage-free, with hope restored, and prepared for your purpose. However, if you refuse to forgive, you have just tied God's hands, stifled your growth, and forfeited your acceleration to His purpose for your life. Remember the words of Matthew 6:15:

"But if ye forgive not men their trespasses, neither will your Father forgive your trespasses."

Next, you must commit to a consistent study of the Word of God. I am not referring to quickly skimming over the scriptures so you can check that off your to-do list. I am talking about deliberately seeking to understand what is taking place in the passages, who is speaking, who is the audience, and what issue is being addressed. Most importantly, ask the Holy Spirit to show you how the passage applies to your own life. Your ultimate question should be, "What does God want me to DO with this information?" James 1:22

"But be ye doers of the word, and not hearers only, deceiving your own selves."

I must tell you, when you get to the point where you realize you need God's Word for your very sustenance, it is life changing. I made the study of the Word my priority. I spoke to no one on any given day until I first heard from God. There were days I missed the mark, but not many. He was first. I found that if I took the time first thing in the morning to pray, sit with Him, study His Word, and express gratitude,

He prepared me for whatever the day would bring. He even guided me through my hard decisions and told me exactly how to handle whatever life threw at me. I began getting stronger as my independence weakened. I began to see dependence on God as my greatest strength, and it opened the door to untold blessings.

Purpose, Purpose, Purpose!
Now that we have walked through the process of redemption, it is time to get to the discovery of your purpose. For me, this required careful consideration of the following questions:

1. What am I good at?
2. What stirs my soul or gives me chills when I see someone else doing it?
3. What comes naturally for me and provides a sense of fulfillment?
4. What have I consistently heard others say that I do well?

This is only a starting point, but with the help of the Holy Spirit you will be well on your way to discovering God's purpose for your life. One thing I warn against is putting limits on God. There are things you probably do almost daily that you have not recognized as a spiritual gift. For example, if you are a person who has the ability to show compassion and care for others without prejudice, you may have the gift of mercy. Do you know that not everyone has a heart with this posture? It is a gift.

After your gifts, talents, and abilities have been identified, the next step is creating opportunities to use what you have been given to bless the lives of others. No gift is given for self, but for the edification (building up) of others. I once knew a minister who was upset because he did not have opportunities to preach in his home church as often as he wanted. I asked him why he didn't seek out other opportunities to share the Gospel outside of church? There are people in prisons, nursing homes, etc. that need to hear God's Word, and they cannot physically attend traditional church services. Why not take the church to them? There was a lady who believed she did not have any spiritual gifts at all. However, she was an outstanding cook. I suggested that she prepare meals for elderly persons in her neighborhood, and when she blessed them with the natural food for the body, she could also bless them with food for their soul while sharing a verse of scripture with them and showing the love of Christ. The sky is the limit, and the only limitations on the use of your gifts are those you create yourself. We must learn to think outside of the four walls of the church building. Jesus' ministry was among the people in the cities and towns which He passed through. The ministry of the Body of Christ is outside of Sunday services. We congregate on Sundays for corporate worship, fellowship, and edification. Once we are strong, we are fueled for the remaining six days of the week, where we carry out the work of our ministry.

The Lord showed me that I had the gifts of teaching, preaching, generosity, mercy, patience, hospitality, administration, leadership, counseling, writing, and helps. Trust me, you will discover that you also have many gifts. What is interesting is that most of these skills and abilities had been operating in my life since childhood, I just never recognized them as gifts from the Lord to be used to help others. As God brought me to purpose, He caused me to pay attention to the details of my interactions with others. The Holy Spirit showed me when certain gifts were in operation so I could see the blessing passed on to the receiver. This encouraged me more than anything else in my life. I love helping people.

I found an opportunity to volunteer for a Hospice organization. I became a Chaplain apprentice, and it wasn't long before I had my own clients. I would visit them, share scripture, pray, and offer to do a task as simple as opening their blinds. I counseled their family members and encouraged them with the love of God. Believe me, your own recovery process will accelerate once you stop focusing on yourself and focus on the needs of others. I always hoped to write a book someday and that "someday" came in August 2019 when my first book was released, *Divorce Journey- God Used My Pain for His Purpose*. This was a dream come true for me.

I entered college just before my 49th birthday to obtain my Social Work degree, and I will have that credential in about eighteen months. This degree will give me access to people that have basic needs while providing opportunities to counsel. Most importantly, I will be able to tell them that there is a God in Heaven who loves them, died for them, and cares about their life. I realize that I will need a unique environment to share the Gospel of Jesus Christ with my clients. I am not at all worried about that. God has a place for me that is currently awaiting my arrival. I know He created me to preach good tidings to the poor and assist them with natural needs. He confirmed my purpose in a dream where He took me all the way back to elementary school. He was a tour guide and showed me all the times where I supported the underdog or tried to befriend the ones that others rejected. I always had a heart for society's outcasts.

If you are broken, bring God the fragments that remain because it is excellent building material for the God of resurrection. Nothing you have gone through will be lost because He has a way of knitting all things in our lives into a pattern for good (Romans 8:28). Maintain a consistent prayer life, be honest with yourself, and allow the Word of God to transform your mind. Do the work because redemption is yours, and like Job, you will eventually be able to shout, "...*I know that my REDEEMER LIVETH...*" (Job 19:25a).

About
Cathy R. Hendrix

Evangelist Cathy R. Hendrix has enjoyed a 38-year journey with the Lord. She serves Him by teaching and preaching the Gospel, counseling, and coaching women through life's hardships. She is the mother of two married daughters and has five grandchildren. She has worked in the Administrative field for 36 years and looks forward to retirement in the new future. After completion of her BSW degree, she plans to dedicate her time to assisting the less fortunate. She published her first book, *Divorce Journey*, in July 2019, which can be purchased from yahscribe.com or Amazon. She has extensive public speaking experience and is using her gifts for the building of God's Kingdom.

For speaking engagements and other public appearances you can reach Cathy at the details below.

(248) 378-7323 | newbeginning27@gmail.com

OBEDIENCE MY PATH TO FORGIVENESS

LINDA HUNT

Brokenness can come in many shapes, forms, and circumstances. It can be disappointment over a situation you had high expectations for. It can come from being hurt or wounded by someone you didn't expect. The picture you had in your mind didn't end the way it started. You ask yourself the question, how did this happen? Yes, life is full of twists and turns, ups and downs, high and lows, and the only coping method you have at times is to suck it up and keep moving.

I can honestly say I have endured some situations where I should have lost my mind. I was heartbroken with nothing or no one to fix me but God and His Word. I'd lay awake at night, praying for daylight to hurry up and come. The darkness seemed so long, and it was like the darkness that plagued my soul. My soul was hurting badly and in desperate need of repair. How do you heal a wounded and broken heart? Where is the wound? What kind of medicine does one take for a broken heart?

The Wedding Rehearsal
It all started about five years after our divorce when my ex-husband asked me to remarry him. After praying and giving it careful consideration, I said yes. He had begun coming to the church I was attending in his desire to court me again. I had given him the boundaries of our current relationship, although we had been married previously. I made it clear he would not have any marriage privileges until we were married again. We were going to Bible Study and Sunday Services together. He was a Deacon, and I was an Adjutant or Armor bearer to my Pastor. We were both serving in the house, and things seemed to be going well.

We shared our desires with our Pastors and began marriage counseling. After one year of marriage counseling, we started planning a wedding date. After setting the time, of course, all the plans for that day were full steam ahead. Little did I know that all those plans were going to come to a screeching halt, and the rehearsal night was what I called the beginning of my trip through hell. He showed up to the rehearsal just as it was ending, and we were ready to go home. I was concerned as to why he was taking so long. My Pastors asked us to come aside to find out exactly what the problem was. It was then he stated he was not quite ready, and he wanted to postpone the date and give it more time. My Pastors, of course, agreed and asked if we would continue working through the decision and come to a final agreement. I knew deep down inside it was not going to happen.

I was in a state of shock and disbelief. I just could not understand why this was happening to me. I cannot tell you how embarrassed and humiliated I was. I began telling my wedding party the wedding was being postponed and feeling so disappointed after they had invested money in their dresses, tuxedos, and all their accessories. I, too, made a substantial investment in a beautiful wedding dress that was in the process of being finished, a cake, along with all the additional accessories. I was left wondering how I was going to explain this to all the people who brought me gifts? I sent invitations out weeks ago to the people that were planning on coming from out of town. I was left shaken and felt so alone as I left the rehearsal to return home, making calls, and telling family and friends the wedding was off!

The Other Woman
I soon found out why he was not ready; there was another woman involved that he had been secretly seeing. I felt in my spirit there was something he was not telling me, but he never said he did not want to get married. After all, he was the one who came and asked me to remarry him. I was in such a state

of confusion and found myself unable to process why God would allow this to happen. I had prayed and believed that God had given me the okay to remarry. We went through twelve months of counseling, had the blessings of our Pastors, and everything seemed to be fine until it all came crashing down in a single night.

Well, the wedding was off, the relationship was over, and he went on to have a relationship with this other woman, and soon left the church. I did find out later that this woman was fifteen years younger than him and was able and willing to satisfy the sexual appetites he knew was off-limits with the two of us. I was hurt, but I was not willing to compromise. I was not ready to give up the relationship that I had with the Lord for a few fleeting moments of pleasure. I had been frank with him; I had to learn to love him again because our first marriage was not the greatest. We had been together for nine years and married for seven years, and during that time I had seen the changes he had made, which led me to believe things were going to be different. He never had any biological children, as he always considered my daughter as his daughter. I continued as best I knew how to go on with my life and pick up the fragments. But I was broken and did not know how to begin the repair process. I knew my mind, heart, and soul were in desperate need of help to make it through this.

Brokenness is probably not the best description to describe how I felt. I almost believe I had stopped feeling. I was numb. I was in a state of disbelief, and I felt so betrayed, so worthless. Suicidal thoughts plagued my mind every day. Many Sundays I would sit in the church services and just cry, asking God to help me. I was hurting badly. I remember when I found out he was going to marry her; I was stunned and hurt. I asked myself, how could he do this to me? He promised me things would be different. It seemed so surreal. I had to be dreaming! This was a nightmare, and I needed somebody to wake me up!

A Wounded Heart

There were so many lonely nights. I would hate to see the night come. I could not sleep; all I could do was lie awake and pray. How do you heal a wounded and broken heart? What type of doctor does one go to? What kind of medicine can he prescribe? At the same time, you are dealing with bitterness and unforgiveness because you're hurting and can't fight back. You have read what the Word of God says about unforgiveness and resentment, and you are shouting, why God? Why? I am human too! Can't you see I am also hurting?

I said some horrible things in my hurt and pain regarding this relationship because it was the source of my pain. I was hurting, and I wanted them to feel the same hurt I was feeling. They went on and planned a big wedding, everything that I would have wished for. Then, to add insult to injury, they even invited some of my friends and church members to the wedding! Talk about a real slap in the face. This marriage was her first marriage. I was his second wife, and she made sure she had all the things a Bride should have. I went into a state of depression, just trying to make sense of it all. I continued on with my life, praying and hoping this nightmare would be soon over, but it wasn't. It was just the beginning! I have never been a vindictive person, but what followed was going to be the ultimate test for me.

The Challenge to Run

A short time after their marriage, they began coming to the church. I was embarrassed and in pain inside because the whole congregation knew our story. Each Sunday, they came in late for everyone to see. I wanted to leave on many occasions, but I knew I could not run. It left me wondering why were they coming here? I had to face this test, and she could not win. No, not this time! You will not win! The challenge to leave was one of the hardest challenges of my life. I cannot tell you it was easy, but I made it through. You can't always run from your hurts and disappointments; you have to fight them through, or you will keep on running. The very thing you are running from is the thing He will use to heal you and make you whole. I had to be honest. I had a spirit of resentment and bitterness that I did not know what to do with. I was angry. I felt I had a right to be angry. How could he agree to come to this church knowing what he had done? I felt like they were out to destroy me. Why was no one able to see my hurt and pain? Why was no one concerned about me and my mental state? Did anyone care? Could anyone notice I was dying on the inside? I felt this was one battle I was in all alone.

After coming to the church for several months, I guess she had her fill and decided to stop coming. I was relieved to be able to breathe again and not having to feel so exasperated every Sunday when I came home from church. It was no longer the source of joy, peace, and comfort I once knew. I never was comfortable the whole time they were there because she always made her presence known. She was going to make sure that I saw her.

Time to Forgive
Shortly after they had been married for five years; my ex-husband called me a few times and asked how I was doing and how was my daughter doing? I would say we were doing fine. I would make sure our conversation stayed neutral because now he is a married man. We talked for a few minutes and hung up. But the second time he called, and before he hung up, I told him, "I have something I want to say." I said, "God put it on my heart if I have the opportunity to talk to you again, tell him you're sorry." He was shocked! "Why are you apologizing to me? I should be apologizing to you. I know things did not go the way they should have, and I am sorry." I said to him, "No, I want to ask you to forgive me because of the terrible things I thought or said about you and

your wife. I want to ask you to please forgive me, and if you get an opportunity to tell her, let her know I am sorry too." I said to him forgiveness is not for you. It is for me so I can have the real husband God has for me. He was quiet on the other end of the phone. He finally said, "You plan on getting married again?" "Of course, I am." That was six weeks before "The Call" and the beginning of how God was going to help me to love and forgive genuinely.

The Last Call

As I was helping my Pastor relocate her office to a larger space in the church, the telephone rang. On the other end of the phone was the wife of my ex-husband. She called to say he had a massive heart attack and was asking to have his funeral at the church because they did not have a church home. My Pastor said yes. Can you imagine? I felt like I was living a nightmare all over again. Why did she want to have his funeral here? She had her time.

Why again? No God! Not again! Not at the very church, I'm still attending and the place where I come to worship. A place where I come to find peace, pray, and find comfort for my soul. Why here? My mind was racing. I was trying not to seem selfish but why does she want to come here? Hasn't she already done enough? God, please! Are you there? Don't you see what is going on here? How long must I suffer? I remember going home that night in disbelief over knowing that I was going to have to face this woman one final time. I tossed and turned all night, dreading that day.

The day of the funeral was drawing near, and I had mixed emotions. How will I respond to her? How will she react to me? I'm praying, Lord, just help me to get through with all of this. I do not know how much more I can take. I am trying so hard to forgive her and get on with my life. It seems I take one step forward and two steps back. Please help me!

Preparing for the Funeral

It's the day of the funeral, and I am so nervous and tired of this whole scenario. I kept trying to be that person God would have me to be. I just kept going over in my mind, why God? Why did I have to go through this again? Why did I have to relive this pain again? Yes, he is dead, but this pain is very much alive. As I am helping my Pastor robe for the funeral, she said something to me that shook my world. "God spoke to me as I was getting dressed to come to the service; He told me to tell you to serve her."

"What! Wait a minute! Serve her! I don't hate her, but I don't exactly love her either! You know what this woman tried to do to me."

"I know Linda, this is probably the hardest thing that I could ever ask anyone to do, but I believe I heard from God."

For a minute, I could not grasp what I was hearing, and with tears in my eyes I said, "I trust you as my Pastor. You would not ask me to do this if God did not tell you. So, I will do it. I don't know how, but I will do this." I left my Pastor to go and wait for her arrival. Obedience will require testing under some of the hardest situations. Obedience is not always easy, even for some that may be leaders. It becomes a battle between good and evil, right and wrong, yes and no. How does one love the unloving and those who despitefully used you? I knew this was going to take strength beyond my own to help me through this. If God didn't give me the right mindset, it would not be done. This was not the time or place to show her how much I didn't like her or a place for vindictiveness. I knew all this was intentional. Yes, you humiliated me in my territory, but I'm going to serve you. Yes, I will!

I pondered what was God trying to teach me in this whole ordeal? What were some of the lessons I needed to take away from this situation? How was I going to finally recover from all this hurt, pain, and disappointment? How could I show this woman the unconditional love of God? Because, after all, He loved me unconditionally and looked beyond my faults and saw my needs. Now this was my opportunity to do likewise.

The Lessons
There are always lessons to be learned from any situation, and the lessons I learned are invaluable to this day because more lessons are going to come. You need to accept that God is always going to be your Father, and as your natural Father, He is concerned about you and wants what's best.

1. I learned that trouble does not last forever. Although your worst nightmare may be painful, it has an expiration date. The Word says, "*Weeping endures for a night, but joy comes in the morning.*" You are going to laugh again. You are going to smile again. Better days are coming.

2. Through my obedience, the first person I had to forgive was the man I felt wrongly betrayed me. You will learn in those tough moments that if you don't forgive, you are holding yourself captive to that time and place. That person has gone on with their life and left you with all the fragments and the broken pieces. You can and will heal and continue living past that moment. Like a piece in a puzzle, eventually you will find the right piece that goes in the right place, and healing takes place.

3. Not forgiving and having bitterness has a way of drawing you in and making you sick in your body and mind because of the poison in your heart. Why? You refuse to let go. Asking for forgiveness is not for the other party, it's for you.

4. Bitterness has a way of keeping you rehearsing the situation over and over in your mind. This can hold you captive and stagnated for years. It can also keep you from those things God has for you in the future. I had to forgive if I ever hoped to be the woman for the true man that God has for me, and not bleed on someone who didn't cause the wound. The injury is gone, but the wound is still there. You must heal and say yes, there was an injury, but you can only see my scar. The scar is to remind you that you lived past the pain and did not die. Every time you want to feel sorry for yourself, just look at your scars and say, "I made it through the test and the mess."

5. It was the obedience that set me free and placed me on the pathway to my forgiveness. I had to trust that my Leader was looking out for my good and not my demise. I needed to pass this test. How many times do we miss the chance to obey what our hearts and minds are telling us? I know this relationship, and the man is not the right person for me. I know this disease is because I am not obeying my body, having an intimate relationship with someone, and I am not married. Or, I am not listening to my body, eating the wrong things, and I have hypertension or sugar diabetes.

6. I had to choose in the face of adversity, and I decided to set my feelings aside that day. I didn't have another day. I had to make a choice that day. The Bible says to choose you this day. You have to make hard choices. I know they are not easy, but the reward is so great. Well, I choose obedience; with tears in my eyes I decided to

obey the voice of the Lord. It was a tough decision, but I thought to myself, this is going to be my day of deliverance. After this funeral is over, I will be free from all the remembrance of the past pain and hurt. I can finally end this chapter of my life that has caused so much pain on one hand but brought so much freedom in another way I did not expect.

Who would expect that a funeral could bring you deliverance and freedom? It was to be the day that the death sentence someone else thought they were serving me was going to be my day of resurrection. I was getting ready to rise again. That place of depression and suicide, and everything that went with it was getting ready to die and go down into the grave. A death, burial, and resurrection were about to take place. I must admit I wanted to walk out of my Pastor's office that day and never look back. All the pain, feeling as if no one was on my side, the embarrassment and humiliation this ordeal has caused me; but deep down inside, I enjoyed the fact the end was drawing near. I was going to serve her, but more importantly, I was going to be a blessing to her.

The Funeral
So now it was time for the funeral. I watched the limousine drive up, and she and another passenger get out. I took one last big breath. My heart was beating so fast. She walked in the door, not knowing that I was the one who was going to be attending to her that day.

I said her, "Good morning, I am going to assist you this morning. I am so sorry for the loss of your husband and I would like to extend my deepest condolences. If there is anything that I can do, please let me know. If you follow me, we can enter the sanctuary this way." I heard the whispers of some of her friends and family, what is she doing? I found strength from within I did not know from where. I saw the look of shock and confusion on her face. I calmly came alongside to escort her into the sanctuary. As I looked facing her, I said "Follow me," and we slowly walked into the Main Sanctuary for all to see. My obedience is getting ready to set me free BIG TIME!!

"Because of the service by which you have proved yourselves, others will praise God for the "obedience" that accompanies your confession of the gospel of Christ, and for your generosity in sharing with them and with everyone else. (2 Corinthians 9:13 NIV)"

"For if you forgive other people when they sin against you. Your heavenly Father will also forgive you. But if you do not forgive others their sins, your heavenly will not forgive your sins. (Matthew 6:14-15)"

About
Linda Hunt

Linda Hunt, a Kingdom Prophetic gift to the Body of Christ, a Marketplace Minister, CEO of Access Business Consultant, LLC. She is the creator of a weekly broadcast, *The Marketplace Connection*, and has interviewed many guests in the past five years from every sphere of society. She is a published author of *Amen Sister!* and visionary of the anthology, *Gathering the Fragments That Nothing Will Be Lost*. She has a passion for seeing women discover their God-given purpose, using them to bring multiple streams of income.

You can view her weekly broadcast on *Worship Radio International,* Saturday mornings, 11 am on **www.worshipradio.faith**, She is also on the staff of the parent company, *Worship Media Group* and you can see her for all your broadcasting and advertising needs.

(313) 828-7190 | hello@lindahunt.net

www.lindahunt.net

PASSING THE MESSAGE OF HOPE

Karen J. Cheathem

The light in the darkness is the sharing of life experiences where hope, love, pain, and sorrow forms the steps needed to rise above and see the joy of a sunset, with assurance that the sun will rise again in the morning. Some will survive painful experiences and teach others how to trust God in the storm; to see the gift of pain that protects us from Satan's demise, and the blessings of pain that make one stronger as they wait on God to answer.

The journey began on June 8, 1949, while a father and his 13-year-old daughter impatiently awaited the arrival of a baby at Mercy Hospital in Muskegon, Michigan. One of the Sisters on duty that night brought them news that they were unsure if the mother would make it because the placenta had separated from the uterus too soon; and being it was a Catholic Hospital, the child would take priority over the mother.

The response would be loud and colorful with a demanding ending, "She can get another baby, but I can't have another daughter," as the other colorful words echoed, a demand ensued that the mother will receive top priority no matter what. But God had a plan and provided a miracle, so both the mother and daughter survived. The baby would live in many places for the next five months until the grandmother stepped in and found a couple in their 50s that wanted a child. At six months of age, Karen Jean Ford was the name given to this baby girl by her adopted parents, Roy and Agnes Ford.

The struggle to understand
I wanted and expected love from family. If not family, then where should it come from? To desire hugs, smiles, and the feeling of belonging is a natural innate gift from God. To give and expect just a hug or smile, why is that so difficult? Perhaps the road the Lord had chosen for me required total dependence on him and no one else. Maybe I had to endure

the pain of rejection so I would be able to hear the voice of God as he guided me through the storms and ongoing pain, to my blessing. My mother was bitter and angry, but that was never seen in public. All I ever wanted, as far as my memory goes, was to please my mom so she would love me, be accepted by classmates, and have friends.

Focus training – learning to endure
The move from our old neighborhood required my attending a new elementary school that would build hate in me like no other place. The everyday laughter about my clothes and platted hair, black and white saddle shoes, and thick socks caused me to feel unwanted. I was not the only one treated this way, but my misery did not need any company. No matter what they did or said, I never let them see me cry.

I made some friends, but there was one girl who was so mean. My day had come; without warning, she picked up a pair of scissors, cut my skirt and dared me to tell. Of course, when I got home my mother saw the cut and was angry. I never told her what happened and took my punishment with anger and bitterness. The repair was more noticeable than the cut, but I learned how to block out the laughter every day that I wore it until school was out. And then there was the name-calling. I was called a Bastard child because my parents were not married, and told I was adopted because no one wanted me. I was told that my parents left me on the doorstep, and the old people took me in.

After school, I ran home and asked my mother if I was adopted. When she said, "YES!" her face changed, and nothing was ever the same from that day until three days before her death. The wall of anger and bitterness was built, and I could never do anything right. The final act at school was being pushed down the stairs. The pain was so bad it hurt to stand up. I was given medication and daily shots for one week. Prognosis, I would never have children.

Building positive work ethics

The schedule never changed. For as long as I can remember, when school was out, I could be found working in the Cherry, Blueberry, Beans, and/or Onion fields. This was a given, not only for me but most of the families in our area. Stay at home mothers would take their children to the fields to earn extra money to buy clothes, shoes, and school supplies for the coming year. My expectations changed when I started Junior High. Picking season began around June for Cherries, followed by Blueberries through mid-August.

My goal was to pick 25 lugs of Cherries – (1 lug equals 25 pounds) per day. We were paid $.50 per lug and a $.05 bonus if you worked all season. Blueberries – I had to pick 15 pails or more per day. The only question that was never asked, "Why do I have to pay mom for lunch when I work, but it is free when I go to school?" My mother no longer drives to the fields, but I was permitted to ride with the neighbor. We had so much fun. I never achieved my goal for cherries, but I exceeded my goal for blueberries and came out financially ahead.

Looking back, I learned one key point, count the cost. The cherry trees were bigger and had more fruit than the blueberry trees, but it required finding a ladder or climbing the tree to pick the berries at the top and moving the lugs as you worked. The blueberry trees were shorter, and the tractor stopped to pick up your berries. This gave you more time to focus on making money.

Mother's Rules:
1. Set your clock, fix your lunch, and lay out your clothes the night before.
2. Do not wake up the family.
3. Arrive early so you have a seat.
4. Show respect to your elders.
5. Do a day's work for a day's pay.
6. Break the rules and the punishment will be severe.

It's funny how the fear of failure can build an enduring positive routine that God can later use to open doors beyond what I could ever hope for as an employee.

High School years
Things were going well. My grades were good, and the gym teacher thought I should try out for the Track Team. The question is, will my mother let me play being she had a hard time with the required gym uniform that came to my knees.
I went to tryouts, but my mother showed up and showed out. One must put a period there to keep the focus on the point.

My senior year was a difficult blessing. I only had four classes in the morning, and worked six hours in the evening at the local hospital, training for a Nurse Assistant. The walk was only 2.6 miles and it gave me time to think and practice songs in my head for choir rehearsal so I could teach the parts. But at the end of the shift, I mostly went home.

Where is God? Can he fix my mother? Why does she hate me at home, but put on a smile whenever we go out as if all is well? There were twin beds in her room, why did she make me sleep in the same room with her? Does she think I would steal something? But God would answer all my questions in time.

One day when I came home, she had put up a wall in the living room with a curtain for a door. She said, "This is your room?" I could not show her how glad I was. Finally, my own room to read, study, pray, and it had a window. I was so thankful.

One morning, I was ready to leave when her door opened. She made me wait until everyone was gone before letting me leave for school. With my books, work uniforms, shoes, and homework, I ran as fast as I could. I made it only to see her sitting in the car in front of the school. I ran to class, but the principal called me down because my mother said I had stolen something from home. I opened my locker as the other students watched and laughed.

When I returned to class the students were still laughing. Sitting behind me was a very handsome young man who tapped me on the shoulder and said, "Hey, you couldn't pay me to take you out!" The class broke out in laughter. And yet there were great times when my mother took a group of us to the Bud Billiken Parade in Chicago every year. She was the best, and we had a great time. If only those days would last forever. We sang together and toured the many states. During those times, life was great. The key was to stay on course and do it right the first time. There was never a peaceful moment. And I never knew what to expect.

Once she took me to my grandmother's house, threw my clothes on the ground and asked my grandmother if she wanted me? She could not take me. I picked up my clothes and put them in the trunk, only to be taken to the home where my birth mother lived, but she was sleeping. I did not wake her. It was scary. As I walked back to the car, she said, "See, nobody wants you!" But God had a plan for me. At some point, my death sounded good. I was tired of living.

A new beginning

It was March 1966; I was invited to sing at a birthday celebration for one of the pastor's wives in our community. When I arrived, there was one empty seat. When I sat down, my eyes beheld a handsome man with a smile. He started a conversation, but I told myself not to even think about him. His aunt invited me, and she was friends with my mother. Later she called my mother, and God worked a miracle. Perry Cheathem was permitted to come over. We practiced social distancing as my mother watched us from the mirror in her bedroom.

My senior year, Perry took me to the prom. In June of 1967, I graduated from High School, the two of us were engaged in July, and we married on August 1, 1967. I was so happy. Although I knew nothing about marriage, intimacy, cooking, and the list goes on, he was and is the most caring and loving husband a person could be blessed to share their life with. Then, on June 13, 1968, the Lord blessed us with a son, and we named him Perry Lee Cheathem Jr. So much for the doctor's prognosis about my not being able to have children.

My mother filed for a divorce, dad paid for it, and with a suitcase, a chair, and a lamp, he moved in with us and stayed for a while. To avoid problems, he eventually moved to Jackson, Mississippi where he lived until he died in 1980. My mother was determined to rule our home.

One Sunday evening after church, we stopped to visit her and she called me names because my dress was just below my knee and not to my ankles where she thought it should be. The reason for my short dress was, I had I just had a baby.

Then she started saying cruel things to my husband. He stood up for me, then asked if I was staying or going home. I ran to the door, and for the first time, I felt good, and I felt loved.

There was no end to her abuse, but she was my mother and I always showed her respect. She could no longer stay by herself, and Perry suggested we bring her to our home and care for her. I will never forget his words. Though she never liked him, he said it did not matter; she was my mother, and we will care for her. Perry had a godly love for her, but she chose to go to a nursing home. I visited her daily, but on Wednesday, May 9, 1979, she looked at me and said, "I thought you didn't love me, but I was wrong." Perry said she was making peace. By Friday, she was gone.

Perry helped me to build a relationship with my birth mother once I realized his statement in-fact was the truth. He said you cannot have a love for God and hate for your mother! I said nothing because he did not understand. She gave me away, she never came to see me, despite living in the same town. She was to blame for all my hurt. I said it was not hating, but it sure was not love. His words pierced my very soul with love; he just did not understand. How could he? His Father and Mother were the best. Hugs and love and spending time with them were like a gift from God. To this day, I miss them.

So many emotions, but Perry never gave up until there was peace in my heart. With that, it was easy to care for her as Alzheimer's destroyed her memory, and I faced the barrel of her shotgun as I prepared her medicine one evening. It was the love of God that gave me peace that day, her face changed, and she put the gun away.

Perry was there, he helped me care for her until we had no choice but to move her to a nursing home. We both were there when she died. She heard me say many times, I love you, and before she died, I called her mom. I watched God break and reshape my life with pain and sorrow, oneness, and love; from talking about the blessings to explaining the struggle that it takes to get one to trust again. To dry the tears with clouds of love from Jesus through a godly husband at a time when I could now hear and believe that God had always loved me and would never give me more than I could bear. I would meet my biological father when I was 18, with great expectations that would come to reality in later years. Our love for the Lord would bond us until his death, and I feel the love from my siblings even until today.

God answers my prayer fifty years later

When I started to write my story, I discovered a small spiral notebook. The name on the first page was that of my music teacher from 63 years ago. He had planned to write an autobiography of my mother from 1898-1960. This book somehow found its way to my home where it remained buried all these years. The Lord would use this book to bring me healing and peace for such a time as this.

The handwriting in the book was my mother's and hard to understand. I learned my grandmother's name was Sarah Hubbert. She was 14 years of age when she gave birth to my mother, Agnes Le Blorance, on July 4, 1898. My mother met her father for the first time at age 19, but there was no love for her and none for him. My mother never went to school because she had to care for her sister, Jennie Inez Roughillo, whose father was white.

The spiral notebook was filled plenty painful events in her life. Her need for love, to be wanted, acceptance, and family all sounded so familiar to me. Now I know why she could not love me with the love that I desired. Yet God was preparing me for his service, and the road less traveled would be my teacher.

Looking back, to achieve the goal that God had for me, my mind and body would have to endure the hardships so his love would prevail. Through this writing, I heard the voice of our Lord say, "Jesus loved me. And all my training was out of love because He made me for a purpose.

My training was designed for his will to be done and for me to learn how to trust and obey."

Lessons from life teachers:
    My fathers, the action of love, and the forgiveness of love.
    My mothers, the pain without love, and to love and give matters to the giver.
    My husband, the love of God, never fails.
    My son, God, is faithful.

From the beauty of successful moments to understanding the stairs of pain. From loss and struggle to viewing moments of peace with Jesus. From not understanding to releasing all to his will. From disappointments to helping others find their way to Jesus. Looking back, I would trade nothing for my journey that was designed from the beginning of time. I know my purpose and now have peace. At the time of this writing all my parents are now gone, but before leaving we had the joy of true love, forgiveness, and grace. I had the honor and privilege of serving them and I look forward to seeing them in heaven.

The privilege of pain is never lost, rather it is a stairway to guide others through the narrow journey where the pain is a privilege. My Lord gathered all the fragments of my life and made me whole so I could pass a message of hope to those who will read my story. The writings of my mother, hidden for all these years, answered my many questions of why? But in a moment in time, she knew I loved her, and in my knowing that I have peace.

The pain from my training has healed. Love replaced hate and has now given me a voice to say, the God I serve will never leave you nor forsake you. And you can be sure of that. From the fragments of my life, he added his love, forgiveness, truth, peace, understanding, and a never-failing promise. And remember the handsome young man who said,

"You couldn't pay me to take you out?" Perry and I saw him and his wife at a class reunion. And he asked me out. I graciously said no and thanked my Lord for the protective pain those many years ago.

What about you?
Are you filled with pain from years ago that you just cannot let go? Has anger and bitterness caused you to avoid family and/or friends? How long will you allow anger and/or bitterness to replace the peace and blessing that comes from Jesus? Our body was not designed to bear such problems. He who loved and died for us did not give us that task. We can have peace when we follow the words of Jesus (Matthew 25:14-15).

Jesus knows every pain we feel. If we allow the pain of yesterday to blind us on our daily walk, we will miss the blessings that God has for us. Healing begins when we allow Jesus to remove the bitterness, unforgiveness, hate, desire to get even, and anything that stands in our way of total obedience to him. You would never ask your surgeon to leave infected tissue in your body. So why would you allow sin to strip you of God's gift of earthly healing with an eternal blessing? We have all been hurt at some point in our life. Some warnings help us avoid greater pain. I gave Jesus the fragments, and he gave me love on earth and more to come when I get home. Now is the perfect time to talk to him. He has been waiting to hear from you.

Prayers and love, His servant Karen

About
Karen J. Cheathem

Karen J. Cheathem is a born-again believer who is committed to the excellence of word living – that is, holding to the promise of God and trusting Him in all things.

She believes and teaches the principles of God's word that we are His stewards, and our purpose is to follow the example of Jesus and serve others in need (Matthew 25:31-46).

She teaches Financial Wellness Workshops, the concept of being unique like the Empire State Building, Financial Literacy/Debt Free Living, and Economic Opportunity, and Empowerment for Ex-offenders in Transition (EXIT).

Former Accounting Instructor Baker College and retired Benefits Analyst Muskegon County. Married to Perry for 52 years; they have one son, Perry Jr., a daughter-in-love, Chris and five grandchildren. However, most important are these seven words KAREN IS A SERVANT OF THE KING!

(231) 728-5490 | kcheathem@aol.com
www.stewardsinaction.com

THE ART OF
REINVENTION
HEALING FROM THE
INSIDE OUT

Tanya R. Bankston, MA, LLPC

The Change Doula

If I could go back in time, there are so many things I would like to change. As a woman now in my early 50s, things like high school graduation, the prom, my first wedding day (I have had three different wedding days but that is another book), and the birth of my children are all good memories. But there are so many other memories I would like to erase such as being molested, being raped at knife point, being the victim of domestic violence, and the many men I have been sexually active with; these are just a few of those memories that I would erase. I have spent decades of my life being ashamed and embarrassed about the poor decisions I made.

In the last ten years, I have taken an evaluation of my life and realized that I needed to REinvent myself. The question then became, how does a person reinvent themselves? What are the tools? Where do you start? What do you do? How can you recapture lost time and opportunities? How do you erase the guilt and shame? How do you begin seeing yourself as important and valuable, or just begin the process of accepting yourself? All these questions became the beginning of my reinvention, but to begin I had to end life as I had previously known it. The chaos, the confusion, and the hidden pain that connected me to my painful past had to be brought into the open for others to see, and I had to acknowledge my need for healing. This is a brief glimpse into that journey.

Starting this process was difficult! I had to come clean, I had to stop hiding and lying. I had to stop pretending that I was okay, when in fact, I was messed up. The biggest catalyst for my change was my need for the relief from the pain in my soul. One morning I looked in the mirror and didn't know the person looking back at me. I remember going to work that morning and getting lost in my mind. I don't even remember the drive to work, I just remember feeling like cattle on the way to slaughter. I felt like I was being herded along without thought. In fact, the entire workday was a blur. The biggest takeaways from that day were bits and pieces of others in the workplace expressing how I secretly felt. "I hate it here," "It's us against management," "It's no use complaining, no one will listen," "I just come here to get a paycheck, I don't care what they do." How could so many people be so unhappy in the same place? How could they know that I was feeling the same way? It was like they were reading my mind and saying my thoughts out loud? My mind was playing tricks on me! Of course, they were not reading my mind! They were dealing with their own unhappiness, but to me everyone was happy and lived a fulfilled life, except me!

I was depressed and felt lost. My life had no value and no meaning. But how did I get here? More importantly, how could I change it? I could not possibly live this lifestyle for 30 or 40 more years, then die without leaving any kind of a mark indicating that I had ever been here! What made matters worse was when I went home, there was more of the same feelings of emptiness! I was a single mother, and my sons needed me to provide food, shelter, and other necessities, but I was unfulfilled. My sons were my only joy, and they kept me moving forward when I wanted to give up!

I needed help to relieve my symptoms of pain, I needed help resolving my conflict, and I needed help to understand why I was so unhappy! This was my first pivotal moment. I needed to change my life! I wanted so desperately to live a fulfilling and meaningful life, but I felt trapped in a dead-end job and in a dead-end life. Changing my life was desired but I wasn't willing to do the necessary work just yet, and I had to experience more pain before I became motivated enough to stop living in the chaos that became my norm. I became self-aware of the need to change but not motivated enough to change.

STEP ONE: Get Tired

STOP LYING...there is a need for change!
My first step was to STOP LYING! I had to stop lying and pretending that everything was okay! I had to stop wearing a painted-on make-up pretty face with a bleached whitened smile that made others think I had it together, and that I was living a life filled with happiness! My first tool for my reinvention was gut level honesty. I was mentally, and emotionally sick! I had years of dysfunction staining my soul. My soul was suffering from so many black eyes and broken bones that I believed it was normal.

Let me give you a few more examples, I started out with a spirit of rejection. My mother got pregnant with me at the age of sixteen. She was unmarried, and during that time there was a lot of shame associated with having children outside of marriage. Reality television did not exist then, in fact, the reality was that when a teenage girl got pregnant, she was usually shunned and sent away to have the baby. The baby was then placed up for adoption or she was forced to have a back-alley abortion.

My mother told me that she considered aborting me but decided against it when the procedure was explained to her in detail. Although I was 16 or 17 when my mother shared this information with me, I felt it should have never been shared. I felt out of place growing up. Armed with this information, it became clearer why I never seemed to fit in.

My parents were forced to get married. My father was a few years older than my mother and had already been in and out of jail and abused drugs, according to my momma. My mother shared with me that my father was verbally mentally, and physically abusive to her and me as a little toddler. My father abandoned my mother with me, and my younger brother.

As a child none of those details mattered to me. All that mattered was the fact that my father wasn't there, and my twisted understanding that I was the reason that he left. For years I felt rejected and angry all the time. Looking back, I questioned how much of that rejection was valid and what percentage was me projecting my thoughts and attitudes about myself onto others?

As a young adult I began seeking to fill in the gaps by looking for love in all the wrong places and for all the wrong reasons. I had the need to be validated, appreciated, celebrated, and not just tolerated. My need for validation led to my developing into a "people pleaser." I would do almost anything to be accepted. I say almost because even though I was a people pleaser, I wasn't a follower. I had strong leadership potential and marched to the beat of my own drums (even though my beat was offbeat and chaotic). There were some things that were absolutely off limits. I started experimenting with drugs and alcohol, but never got into heavy experimentation. There were too many times that I needed to be in control, and I was not able to be in control while under the influence of drugs.

My drug of choice became sex as a means of finding someone to love and accept me. Although I was promiscuous, I at least felt like I had control over my life (I was telling myself more lies). I began sleeping around and justified my actions behind the lie of expressing myself sexually and learning to exercise my independence. My actions caused me to spiral out of control emotionally. I began living a life where I became bitter, cold, and callous. I had the capacity to see weakness and flaws in others, but I ignored my own need for change! As I developed a greater need for validation and acceptance, I developed a greater need for control. As I developed this greater need for control, I lost more control over my emotions and my need for closeness from others. As this desire for love grew, I pushed others away. It became a never-ending circle; push people away and seek more sex to feel closeness from others. Each time I had sex, it provided less fulfillment but my desires for more sex increased and intensified. With every sexual encounter and every failed relationship, I was separating myself from God. I was searching for something that I would never find by changing sexual partners. I was searching for LOVE. It was difficult to overcome searching for love, especially through sex. Sex is not love and love is not sex.

In order for me to change in this area I sought out help through counseling with the pastor at my church, I sought out help through reading all kinds of books on self-esteem, self-acceptance, and self-confidence. I sought out help from a professional Mental Health Counselor (this became the impetus for my decision to become a Licensed Professional Counselor). Each of these resources helped me in a tremendous capacity, but my greatest strength came from searching for help in the Bible. I began studying and meditating on scriptures that dealt with God's love for me. Meditate means something different to everyone but here I am, speaking of reading, deciphering, and memorizing each scripture until it began resonating in my spirit.

Let me give you two examples. Luke 12:7 indicates, *"Don't be afraid; you are worth more than many sparrows. ... So don't be afraid; you are more valuable to God than a whole flock of sparrows. ... "But every hair of the hairs of your heads is numbered, therefore you shall not be afraid, because ..."* I used this scripture to help me with my poor self-esteem and poor body image to help me heal as I came to understand that I am beautiful in my imperfections to God. I learned to silence my inner critic and stood in front of the mirror for months, saying, *"I am more valuable to God than I can comprehend. God took his time forming me and the very hairs on my head are numbered."*

A second scripture that I stood in the mirror and recited a million times was Psalm 139:14 *"I will praise You, for I am fearfully and wonderfully made; Marvelous are Your works, And that my soul knows very well."* I told myself over and over again, "I am a marvelous work. My soul knows this, and this includes my mind and my emotions. God says I am wonderful! I am wonderful!" Of course, I didn't feel wonderful and I didn't see anything wonderful in the mirror, but I continued until I believed it. I taped messages all over my house. I taped them in my car, I wrote them over and over, and over again on index cards, in my journal, and I started telling these affirmations about myself to other people. I took a tape recorder and recorded my voice then played it on rewind over and over while I slept to let the messages sink into my mind without interference. I am sure people thought I was crazy! My new attitude was, if I can repeat and rehearse negative messages that others say and think about me, then surely, I can repeat and rehearse positive things about myself! I had gotten tired of being tired!

STEP TWO: Get Tired of Being Tired

Rewind, Repeat
All my fragmented relationships never added up to a complete whole, healthy, relationship. These relationships could never become a healthy relationship, first because I was broken, and second because I could not attract partners who were healthy and whole. When I did attract a healthy man, I was not attracted to him for various insignificant reasons. I expected and searched for someone to complete me, love me, and make me whole. I was seeking validation outside of myself. My brokenness was a magnet for other people who were either broken themselves, or predators who preyed on broken people. It didn't matter which were broken and which were predators, I couldn't distinguish between the two, and I interpreted their behavior for love.

I was tired of being tired, but I still didn't know what change should look like for me, or if it was possible to change. It was also at this point in my life where I wasn't quite sure that I needed to change. I was at a point in my life where it became easier to blame others than to take responsibility for my own behavior. I had not yet grown to the maturity level it takes to be responsible for my life choices and my life outcomes. I was still willing to allow my need for nurturing, protection, and love to be the responsibility of others rather than taking on the responsibility for myself.

Secretly, it felt good to blame momma and daddy for screwing up my life. My life had become a living wasteland, filled with rotting soul-ties, and the twisted carnage of past male relationships. I had no expectations of getting married because I didn't trust men. I saw most men as liars, cheaters, and perpetrators of abuse. The only exceptions to my perception of these distortions were my uncle, my cousin "Brother," and my great uncles.

My experiences outside of these relationships had proven all other men to be liars, cheaters, and abusers. My uncle, cousin-brother, and great uncles were the only men I saw as safe, fun, and providers for their families. I understood that other men wanted something for their affection, protection, and provision. I learned this lesson early.

My first experience of being molested was at the age of six or seven by a family "friend." I remember he was a victim of abuse. As an only child his mother beat him, and verbally abused him regularly. I recall his mother being a heavy drinker, and she was so mean to him all the time. But why did that cause him to sexually abuse me? I told no one about him molesting me, in fact, I blocked it out for years! I learned at the age of six or seven about perversion. It would be more than four decades before I learned how to heal from this perversion, and the connection between this early childhood exposure and my confusion with love and sex. This change was not easy nor was it quick. I was able to use some simple techniques to make changes in my life. Oftentimes we look for complicated answers for complex problems when we should be looking for simple solutions to complex problems.

One tried and true technique for taking responsibility for your own happiness is to begin taking an assessment of where your life is currently. When things seem to be working in your favor, assess who is there in your corner celebrating you, and when times are difficult or you hit your rock bottom, take an assessment of who is there in your circle helping you clean up the mess from your chaos.

I learned the hard way that not everyone in your circle is in your corner. There will be way more people celebrating than there are when it is clean up time. When all the fanfare is over, can you look at yourself honestly in the mirror and make the decision to change your life? Once you make the single decision can you continue taking steps in the direction to change? It will not be easy; it seldom is, especially if you are like I was and enjoyed blaming others for your poor life choices.

Sure you can blame your parents, your educational background, genetics, your racial background, your economic status, and a long list of other things, but the truth of the matter is that you are responsible for the outcome of your life. You had no control on where you started but you can control where you end. No one else can be blamed for your life choices and no one else can take credit for your success. It starts with a decision to CHANGE!

STEP THREE: CHANGE!

Change is NOT always immediate

When I share my three-step process of change with my clients, I always emphasize the simplicity of three steps, BUT it is NOT EASY! Actually, the most difficult step, in my opinion, is step two. This is where the most work is done because it is an active step. Constant, consistent, concise execution of the change process is needed.

Step two sometimes requires you to repeat step one, the decision. Step two is a natural segue way into step three, but it is not linear, and may cause you to vacillate several times before realizing that you have changed. Let me give you a real-life example that I experienced. When I was in an abusive relationship, I felt trapped and stuck, believing I was destined to die in that abuse; and based on statistics alone there is a huge possibility that I would have! In fact, I was often told, "If I can't have you no one will. I will kill you first." I believed in my heart that every threat was sincere. When he put the loaded shotgun to my head and pulled the trigger, twice, I know the only thing between me, and death was my answered prayer!

Once I got out of the situation, I vowed to never allow myself to be victimized again. I got mental counseling, I went to a support group, and I read everything I could on domestic violence (DV). I didn't know I changed my attitudes towards dating until I got over my fear and trauma of the DV. Once I decided to date again after several years of being single, I discovered that I CHANGED!

I made a conscious effort to envision the type of man who was deserving of me. I listed on paper the types of character traits that were valuable to me. There were some no-matter-what qualities that I am not willing to compromise such as respect, loyalty, and being violence free. I had a certain physical attraction, but the main emphasis was character.

Step three is both a celebration step to acknowledge you changed behavior and a management step to continue that behavior. Step three requires diligence to continue to honor and uphold the new change processes you have put in place for your life. Step three requires your continual improvement, and dedication to your REinvention. Step three is a lifelong commitment to shift your paradigms as often as you need, to become greater than the person you were before. Step three is living what you believe and saying what you envision for your future. Step three is a daily journey to healing from the inside out. As you heal, step three will become a public display of the inward manifestation of the Living Masterpiece you have become.

About
Tanya R. Bankston

While many struggle to keep their heads in the game, Coach Tanya Bankston helps clientele worldwide leap over hurdles and successfully cross the finish line—many times, with minimal sweat and tears. Out of the shadows of abuse, low self-esteem and trust issues, Bankston pushes clients to discover and cultivate the leader within. Complete with her no-nonsense coaching style, zero tolerance for excuses and passion for reinvention and repurposing, Bankston inspires women to transition from simple existence to living a life of abundance—unapologetically. From abandonment of her father, molestation, and date rape—to domestic abuse, welfare dependency and divorce—she's no stranger to the struggle. But she has made a conscious choice to walk as a victor, not a victim. As a certified life, leadership and solutions-focused coach, Bankston trains her clients to not only develop stellar products and services, but quality relationships—relationships that position them to stand out and soar in the marketplace. In addition to her coaching certification from the Universal Coach Institute, she also holds two Master's degrees one in Mental Health Counseling, and another in Leadership. She has a Bachelor's degree in Community Development and Health Science, and a graduate certificate in Human Resources from Central Michigan University. As the president and CEO of Greater Heights Coaching & Professional Development LLC, she encourages clientele to reach higher, achieve more and live their best life now! Her signature team-building workshops have encouraged audiences from D.C. to Kansas City, offering them key tools on negotiations, collaboration, compromise, and communications. Founded in 2009, offers both corporate and team-building activities for business professionals of all backgrounds. Together with her educational background, corporate tenure and passion to drive others to succeed, she's on a definitive mission to positively impact the lives of all she comes in contact with— taking them from good to great! Unlike the average life coach, who coaches clients to become better at what they do currently, Coach Bankston encourages her clientele to radically reinvent themselves opening the door to a myriad of opportunities. Just because a team has a coach does not mean they win. Let Coach Bankston catapult you to your next best level of success— fostering change through the pursuit of personal and professional excellence.

For speaking engagements or to schedule your next coaching experience,

(866) 733-3654 | CoachTBankston@mail.com
www.CoachTBankston.com

LOVE MADE ME DO IT

Meskerem (Meski) Mekasha

When we found out I was going to be a mother, it was the happiest day of my life. The joy was overwhelming. I was so ready to be a mother; to love, to protect, to give him or her the unconditional love I had gotten from my own mother; it was a dream come true. It happened; naturally, I felt so blessed. On my first trimester, I couldn't keep anything down. The morning sickness kept me in the bathroom for hours. It got to the point I was not able to go to work. A few weeks later, I was not able to eat anything, and my mouth was sore from throwing up so much. My new bedroom was in the bathroom. I spent countless nights on the bathroom floor. I was so skinny you could see my bones through my clothes. I was a skeleton, weighing eighty-nine pounds.

I made an appointment to see my doctor. I wanted to make sure everything was okay with my baby, not so much about me. When she saw me, she was horrified at how skinny I was, so she sent me to the hospital so they could give me an IV. They kept me overnight. When I got home, my doctor called to check on me and see how I was feeling. When I told her, I was feeling the same, she said she wanted to connect me with a naturalist who could help me.

The following day I met with her. To my surprise, I had to get hooked up with tubes filled with vitamins, minerals, protein, and everything else I needed to make it throughout my pregnancy. I had to carry all this around for a long time. My visiting nurse came in every other day to change the bags.

It was so challenging being with other people or going anywhere because, on top of carrying a bag, I needed to hold a cup to spit in since I was not able to swallow. For the first and second trimester, I was miserable. I used to cry a lot. I was at home, unable to do anything. This was the new normal for me. Can I go through it? Am I going to have a healthy baby? The constant doubt was fighting inside of me; I had to remind myself God is going to deliver me. I need to put all my trust in him.

When I was thirty weeks, I was admitted to the hospital because my sugar level was sky-high. I needed to take insulin twice a day to stabilize my sugar level, and my body was filled with water. I was high risk, and my emotions were all over the place. After all this, will I be able to give birth to a healthy baby? God, please let me have a healthy baby. I gave it all I have. I am weak, it is all in your hands. I beg you. I was on bed rest day in and day out. I didn't know what to expect after two months of absolute misery.

On Father's Day, my doctor said it was time to push. That was the easy part. I pushed and pushed and pushed, and she said we are almost there, just one more. I went for it and pushed one last time. You did it, my doctor said, "it's a girl!" I didn't care. I was waiting to hear her cry, and I immediately gave thanks to God. Then followed a moment of anticipation, God, please let me have a healthy baby. I am begging you. Then I heard a cry and my heart filled with joy. For nine months I had waited for this labor of love. All the pain I had gone through now is gone. I am holding her and counting ten fingers and ten toes. It is all there, how blessed I am!

Wow, she is gorgeous. Look at her beautiful eyes. I see myself in her. I was in love, and out of nowhere the name Rebecca came in my head. Yes, yes, that is it. Yes, it should be her name, I said to her dad. He said he liked it. After we got home, life revolved around her. She was the best, and she was a loving baby to care for. She slept all night. We got to know each other. I enjoyed being a mother. It was a happy time in our house, and by the grace of God, I was healthy and whole.

I am grateful you gave me everything I wished for, and my promise to you God is, I will love this baby. I will protect her from anyone trying to hurt her. This a gift of life you have entrusted to me. I ask you to guide me in the right direction. I will serve you in all my ways till the end of my time here on earth. Amen.

I went back to work after eight weeks. The first few weeks were the hardest. I missed her so much. I was still breastfeeding, and my new norm was pumping milk two or three times a day while at work. That was not easy in an environment filled with men who do not understand what a new mother goes through. I had to endure scrutiny from my coworkers about the size of my breasts, as well as the leaks coming out of them from time to time. We found a great lady to take care of her during the day. For the most part, life was great. We were one happy family.

When she was six or seven years old, we started having some problems in our marriage. My husband became emotionally abusive. He was always controlling, but I was so busy with my daughter that I did not pay much attention to his behavior until she was a little older. By the time she started first grade, he was complaining that I was never home, even though I had the same schedule for years. I didn't understand why he was acting this way. I tried to reason with him, but it was like talking to a brick wall. Nothing worked. He wanted me to resign from work and stay home. How am I going to do that? I have never depended on anyone for money in my adult life.

After it became clear that he was not backing off from getting what he wanted, for the sake of peace and my family, I resigned. My new life as a stay at home mom was something I had a difficult time getting used to. For a few months, I felt worthless. This is not me. I always managed to provide for myself, and I could not bear asking for money to buy those things I wanted to get. I gave it a lot of thought, and in the end, I couldn't do it. I was miserable. I told him how I felt, and that I desired to go back to work. Even though he did not like it, he knew I was serious, so he agreed.

I started looking for work, and within a week I got a job. It felt so right to be back in the workplace. I was happier, and I got my confidence back. I smiled a lot. I now have so much energy and I was financially secure. My workplace was a lot closer to home, which was a bonus. If I can keep this up, I can touch the sky.

After a long day at work, I was always so excited to be greeted by my child with open arms at the front door. This was the best feeling ever! She would be waiting too, looking at the clock over and over. And he would tell me all the time how she keeps reminding him how long it will be 'till mom gets home?

One morning as I was leaving for work, I could not find my car keys even though I always put them in the same spot. I looked everywhere but I could not find them. He was watching me going crazy and did not move or offer to help. Something is wrong with this picture. Just as I was giving up, I saw the smirk on his face. I knew then he deliberately hid them. That did not sit well with me. I was furious! I was so mad I was shaking. I wanted to punch his face. And to my surprise, he had the nerve to pull the same act again.

He said, "you know, you're going to work is not necessary. If you stay home and take care of your daughter, it will be best for everybody." I was choking with anger and had tears coming down. I cleared my throat slowly and said, "Can I please have my keys?" He started pulling the key out of his pocket, and as I reached for them, he raised his arms up high. He is six feet two while I am only five feet six on a good day with my heels.

He thought this was a joke. Without any hesitation, I picked up my phone and called 911. He was scared that I called the police, and it took him by surprise. He handed me the keys and I left before the police got there. I was so angry I cried all the way to work.

When I got to work, I went straight to the bathroom to clean myself up and calm my nerves. I wanted to just stay in the bathroom and cry all day, but I had work to do. Exactly how am I going to get through this day? I sat at my desk, unable to think. Then I went outside to get some air because I couldn't breathe.

After work, I went home to get a change of clothes and talk to my baby. When I walked into the bedroom, all my belongings were missing. The closet was empty, no clothes, no shoes, nothing, not even a change of underwear. I could not believe my eyes. What happened? As I stood there, I thought perhaps he put them in a suitcase for me, how nice of him. So, I went downstairs and asked him where my stuff was? He said casually, I put it in storage. As I stood there fighting back my tears, I knew I had a choice to make. Should I call the police? Or should I save my daughter from witnessing her father getting in trouble, or should I let it go?

After getting myself a place to stay, I went to get Rebecca and my belongings. He told me they were never in storage, but he put everything in a dumpster. I was devastated. I walked out of his house with nothing. I wanted the divorce to be fast, so I agreed to everything on the divorce papers. No child support, no alimony, no furniture, no dividing of assets – he could keep everything, I just want out! I remember my attorney thinking I was crazy because I did not want anything from him. All I wanted to have was my freedom and being able to raise my daughter the best way I knew how.

We agreed to joint custody; it seemed everything was working out day by day. We become friends and were able to at least be in the same room to attend a parent teacher conference or go to a baseball game. That made my baby happy. We celebrated her birthday together. Life was good until she got to middle school.

Rebecca was playing basketball; she was the tallest girl and was having fun until her dad started acting like he was the coach. The more he pushed her, the more she hated playing basketball. When she was eleven years old, she wanted to go to a sleepover birthday party at one of her friend's houses. I dropped her off and stayed for a few moments then left. A few hours after getting home, I got a phone call from Rebecca, saying her dad was at her friend's house, asking her to go home with him. I asked her to give him the phone, and after a long conversation he left without her.

The next day, he took her phone and all her toys away. When I got there, he had taken the TV out of her room and thrown it out the window. He was screaming so loud I did not think it was safe for her to stay there, even though she was supposed to stay with him this weekend. I could not leave her with him because he was out of control, so she went home with me.

For the next several months, she stopped going to his house from time to time. We would go out to dinner so they could talk and try to find some kind of peace, hoping things could return to normal, but it wasn't working. One night at dinner, Rebecca told him she did not want to go back to his house. He was agitated and left without saying goodbye.

Shortly after this incident I got a call from her principal telling me we needed to deal with some issues that required my presence, so I dropped everything and went to school to talk to her. I was informed that her dad went to school with a few police officers, demanding to search her locker because he thought she might have some drugs. It turned out all she had was some Advil I gave her for menstrual pain. I could not believe he did that. To this day, I do not understand why. After that, he would call me regularly with all kinds of threats about how he was going to get me in trouble. How I will be going to jail, and so forth.

A few weeks later, one morning at work I was asked to go to the reception desk. A few police officers were waiting and wanted to know who I was? When I told them, they said I was served. When I read the letter, it meant he was taking me to court for violating his parental rights, so now I needed to get ready for the fight to love and protect my daughter; that was the promise I made to her when I held her for the first time. And I will never quit.

At the hearing, the attorney explained what was going on, and the judge ordered the two of them to go counseling and appointed someone through the court system. For the next several months, they did intense sessions. In the meantime, Rebecca was preparing to enter high school. There was a great opportunity to attend one of the best high schools in Michigan, The International Academy of Bloomfield Hills.

The school was initially created for the International community. The idea was for foreigners, when they are assigned a position to other counties, to ensure their kids will get the same education no matter where they go, which made it easier for the families. In Michigan, most school districts get a lottery-based opportunity to fill the available space as long as they pass the entry exam, which was extremely hard for our school district.

We had ten spots for all those who passed the entrance exam. Rebecca got number nineteen, so she had to prepare to take the exam and hope for the best, but even if she passed the exam for her to get in line, these other kids either had to fail or withdraw their entries.

They continued counseling three times a week with no progress; one day, while I was waiting in the lounge, I saw him walking out. I could tell he was upset. A few minutes later she came out and I could see in her face that she had been crying. After I consoled her, she told me he did not want to hear what she has to say because the counselor sided with her. He got mad and they had a falling out with the counselor, which is why he left. He then went back to court to get a different counselor, and the judge granted his wish.

In the meantime, it was almost time to go back to school. I did not know where she would attend high school. I was still waiting to hear the results of the lottery. A few days before school was supposed to open, I got a phone call from the school's coordinator, telling me that Rebecca had gotten great results on her exam, and the other nine didn't. She said, "I want to congratulate her and ask if she would like to attend school. It will be an honor to have her attend the International Academy." After I hung up the phone, I was so overwhelmed with joy that I cried for days. I knew this was God answering my prayers. She loved her new school. The two of us were doing fantastic. I was doing everything I could to provide for her, even though it had been extremely tough I knew God had protected me. I was broke financially trying to keep up and there were many days where I did not have any money to buy food because he stopped supporting her. Not only that, every time he took me to court, I had to pay my attorney. It was the hardest time of my life.

For two years, we went back and forth to court. The only time he saw her was when they were in counseling. I tried not to get in the middle no matter what, since he is still her father After he walked out from the second counseling session with his new counselor he went back to court with a different motion, this one involved the school. I got a call from the principal to meet with him. Rebecca told me her dad was trying to sue the school for supposedly breaking the law by accepting a student with a false address. He said she no longer lived with him, but when we got divorced, we had joint custody, so we kept her in the same school.

When she got accepted in high school, it was based on the school district he lived in, so he knew he could win. I could not believe what I was hearing. He wanted his own child expelled from the best school in the United States; a school with a 98% acceptance rate for the top ten colleges. This cannot be true! I was devastated. How could anybody do that to anyone, let alone your own child. I was speechless. How was I going to tell Rebecca this? As I was walking out, she was standing by the door, waiting for me. She heard everything. To my surprise she was okay, consoling me and telling me everything was going to be okay,

The next morning, when I dropped her off at school Rebecca handed me a sealed envelope addressed only to "Judge." When I got there, I gave the envelope to my attorney and let him know it was from Rebecca to the Judge, and it was still sealed. He took it to the back as I was setting on the bench in the hallway, waiting for the courtroom door to open. To my surprise my ex-husband came and sat next to me. I could feel my anger starting to touch my face. I slowly got up and moved about ten feet from him to stand on the corner.

Within a few moments he was standing beside me, so close I could feel his breath on my neck. It was one of those moments where you don't know what to do. I started walking away, filled with emotions, and trying to hold back my tears. I wanted to hide my face from all the people around me.

Then, he came over to me again, this time telling me I should get ready to go to jail. At the time, it felt like a lifetime. I noticed people were starting to enter the courtroom, so I left him standing there and went in. A few minutes later my attorney came and sat next to me. He informed me that he had passed the letter to the judge, so he will be able to read it before he arrived in the courtroom. I was sitting there, trying to come to myself when the bailiff said, "All rise."

To my surprise, we had a new judge, her majesty. After a few cases she called both our names. In her hand she was holding the letter. She looked up and said, "Mr. Scott, is your daughter attending The International Academy?"

"Yes, your honor," he said.
"Your motion today is to get her expelled because she was admitted while living at your residence. Am I correct?"
"Yes, your honor."

She took a few minutes before responding to his motion. "I am well aware of what kind of school your daughter is attending. If that was my own child, I would be so proud that I would let the whole world know. Sir, I don't know what you are trying to do, but if I ever see you in my courtroom again regarding this matter, I guarantee you I will hold you in contempt." With that she picked up her gavel and said, "Case dismissed."

As I was standing there looking at her face, it felt like I was looking at GOD himself sitting on the throne on judgment day. It was one of those moments that live in you. No matter what, you should never lose hope.

About
Meskerem (Meski)
Mekasha

Born and raised in Addis Ababa, Ethiopia, Meskerem (Meski) Mekasha immigrated to the United States at the age of 23. Eventually settling in Michigan, Meskerem built a 20 plus year career in automotive sales.

Meskerem enjoys gardening, engaging in community events, and of course writing. She currently lives with her family in Michigan. This is her debut publication.

(248) 396-9833 | mekasha5@aol.com

THE SECRET IS OUT

HAYDEE IRVING

One of the last memories I have about church was of a pastor preaching about homosexuality being a sin. I was young, but the way he preached the message made me feel grieved because it sounded hateful and condemning. Since I can remember, I have struggled with my sexuality. I was introduced to sex from a very early age, not because I wanted to but because my innocence was taken from me at the age of 6 or 7.

I remember looking at girls from that early age and starting to question what it would be like to be with them. Not because I wanted to but because a seed of perversion had been planted. I went on questioning my sexuality for years until I finally started acting on my thoughts and started to pursue women. I remember feeling so good and yet so lonely. It was like eating dairy, knowing you are lactose intolerant. The more I dibbled and dabbled, the more comfortable I became with the idea of being with a woman for the rest of my life; even if it compromised how I felt internally.

I grew up in a traditional immigrant Hispanic home. My mother was raised in a Catholic home with a single mother. She had to grow up at an early age to help her mother financially maintain a stable home. My father was raised in a strict Pentecostal home. He also had to grow up at an early age to help raise his ten siblings. Neither of my parents were raised in emotionally stable home environments which effected their parenting skills and my own emotional stability.

When I was sexually abused by someone close to the family both of my parents were shocked but then did the whole "hush and don't tell" thing. This confused me because I didn't understand what was happening. All I knew was it was something that should not have happened. After that day, communication got worse with my parents. My dad couldn't look at me for quite some time and my mother was just quiet.

After a while I got used to the no talking thing and that is how my childhood was, internalizing everything. I personally never talked about my feelings and always ran away from caring about anything. Even though I didn't know how to handle my emotions, I would have thoughts about my dying at a young age. That made me not care about my life and I put my life at risk multiple times. I started to drink and do drugs at the age of thirteen, and soon I started to abuse other substances. This continued until I turned nineteen.

At the age of eighteen, I was in a three-year relationship with a woman that I was planning on marrying. We met when I was fourteen and we started as friends. At that time, I started acting on my desires of being with a woman. We would talk every day and I learned that we had a lot of things in common regarding the lack of emotional support with our upbringing. I found safety in her and began allowing her into my space just enough for me to still have control over my feelings and not get hurt. As we moved on with our relationship, I was very passive aggressive and always playing around with her feelings. I was a serious narcissist in the relationship.

It's crazy how much you will do to protect yourself from being hurt. We were both broken people seeking safe places in each other. As we reached year two, she started having more questions about God. At this point I wasn't an atheist, but I definitely did not believe in God. She went to a conference organized by the leader that counseled me. While at the conference she had an encounter with God that changed her life. She brought it to my attention, and I got angry because I knew that meant she would leave me, and I would be alone.

She started to go to church and we avoided the conversations about it. I started to notice that I no longer had a strong attraction towards her. As we reached year three, I was over at her house, and her people were going to church; so, I joined. But I did not join with good intentions.

I went into church with a huge guard up, ready to prove the pastor wrong if she tried to talk me into joining the church. But after my first service, I was intrigued and continued going. I started to question God regarding my desires about wanting to be with women. I questioned why it was wrong according to Him and how I was supposed to get rid of these desires. When I asked these questions, I wasn't expecting an answer back; but God answered all these questions randomly at different services.

My girlfriend and I at the time looked at each other as if God gave the go to end the relationship. As God used the pastor of the church to answer all my questions, I became a believer. I decided that day to end the relationship with my girlfriend. I arrived at her house that night and asked her, "Is our relationship affecting your relationship with God?" She answered with tears in her eyes, "Yes."

We, of course, didn't know how to properly handle the situation and decided that this process would be easier if I moved in. This did not make things any easier. I did not show any emotion regarding the situation and she was drowning in emotions. I felt as if all I needed to do was to stop being with women and start dating a man. So, I did that, but I still felt unfulfilled and it only created more animosity in the situation, so I chose to finally move out. Things only got worse because I still was not understanding what God wanted for my life. God did not just want me to be with a man, he wanted me to be with HIM.

After the breakup I dated two guys who both pretended to want God so they could have a chance with me. I still felt empty, broken, and confused. During this time, the pastor kept asking me to come meet with her. I avoided it of course because I knew I would have to talk about my feelings. But I reached my lowest when I got a call from my ex-girlfriend's mother, telling me that I was banned from coming to the house. At that moment I realized how much I had hurt her. I decided to finally go to this meeting and talk to the pastor.

My experience was with someone trained by the Holy spirit and it was not your typical therapy session. It took me a long time to finally accept the invitation to counseling. But I had to reach my lowest point and I needed help. This meeting did not at all go how I expected. Instead of getting comforted, I got rebuked for being a renegade about people's feelings. You would think I would be angry about that, but instead I was disappointed in myself. I left, recognizing that God was super real. So, I broke up with my boyfriend at the time and ran to God.

I went to a park and sat in the parking lot, crying. I sobbed to God and gave Him my real yes. I went back to counseling, and as I talked about my past experiences, I realized how broken I was and in need of Jesus. A lot of times we get so stuck on what is wrong that we don't see the full picture. I was not just struggling with my sexuality, I was also struggling with abandonment, hurt, betrayal, anger, lust, and so much more.

My struggle with sexuality was just the surface of what was really going on inside of me. I was broken and craving to be loved and did not know it. The first thing we dealt with was the anger I had towards my parents, and disappointment of how things were handled when my innocence was stolen. I felt abandoned, lost, and hurt. In order for me to heal, I had to talk to them and tell them that I forgave them and ask them to forgive me for lashing out in rebellion. I know a lot of times we talk about how forgiving is for us more so than the other person, but in this situation, it was for my parents and me.

My parents were tormented every day after what happened to me. Can you imagine being responsible for your baby, and your baby gets hurt under your roof and you couldn't do anything about it? They felt as if they failed me as parents, and on top of that they were never taught to deal with feelings, so they didn't know how to comfort me. It was not their fault that I was hurt. They were also hurt in this situation by their trust being abused and their child suffering the consequences.

When I came to this understanding, I asked for forgiveness because I rebelled against them and had no respect for them. I disrespected and dishonored them constantly. I hurt them because I was angry. Once the forgiveness took place with my parents, I had to forgive my abusers. I had to let go of the control they had over me and my emotions. Once I forgave them there was still a process of the memories and trauma. Even to this day I am still going through a process of trusting God. Forgiving God was interesting because I didn't know that I had fought against God. I didn't understand that I felt abandoned by God. I felt betrayed because of what I went through. I felt as if God didn't care that I was hurt until one day He spoke to me through a character in the movie, *The Shack*. He spoke to me through how the character felt hurt and abandoned by God. He felt as if God didn't care about his daughter being kidnapped. God came to speak to him and took Him through a journey to show His love for him and how he never desired for him to go through this pain.

There is still evil on this earth. Evil infiltrates to steal, kill, and destroy, but God comes in to interject. After forgiveness took place, I was able to see my experience differently. I saw how God could use my testimony to impact others, but of course there was some uncertainty in me. I didn't know how I was going to be able to minister to those in the LGBTQ lifestyle, or the ones coming out because of how the church presently handles the situation.

According to Gallup News, in 2017, 4.5% of Americans identify as LGBTQ. I believe those numbers have grown by leaps and bounds in the last three years. As this rate keeps going up, the church needs to be prepared on how to minister to those in the LGBTQ lifestyle.

Since I have been saved, I have visited many churches and come to understand that a lot of leaders have not sought to understand those in the LGBTQ community. We need to learn how to meet them where they are and how to serve them with love. I am not at all saying that you have to accept their sin, but you have to know to love them back to Christ.

"Instead, speaking the truth in love, we will grow to become in every respect the mature body of him who is the head, that is Christ. From him the whole body, joined and held together by every supporting ligament, grows, and builds itself up in love, as each part does its work." (Ephesians 4:15-16)

The pastor who helped me through my process impacted my life because she listened and allowed God to do the work. Because of how I saw the church growing up, I assumed she was going to try and cast the devil out of me. That is why I didn't want to give counseling or deliverance a shot. The number one thing you need to take into consideration is that being gay, lesbian, or transgender isn't any more of a sin than stealing, adultery, or not honoring your parents. You must shift your perspective. Who were you before you met God? Why were you a mess before God? And do you truly believe that everyone deserves the love of God? There has to be a level of compassion for those who are not in communion with God because they don't know God! You get to know God; you had the opportunity to experience the delivering power of God, and His unconditional love, so why can't they have the same? We need to be the pioneers who change the way religion has brought division and hurt. We cannot become like the pharisees who told Jesus to not perform miracles on the sabbath. Paul was able to have compassion for those he ministered to because he was one of them. He related to them and then corrected them. Jesus did the same as He ministered to those following Him. Jesus put himself in our place and sacrificed himself so we may be forgiven.

Because the sin of sexual immorality is like any other sin, we know there is a process that needs to be taken after salvation. There is a process of retraining your mind, body, and soul. There are old patterns that need to change, and we need to allow God to have His way with them. Yes, I had counseling, but the majority of my deliverance happened when I was alone with God. The pastor assisted by loving me, listening to me, praying for me, and guiding me through scripture when I had questions. There were a lot of times that I needed to be corrected, but once I reached that place where I fell in love with God, it was easier for me to receive correction.

My process through deliverance was all about my love for God. I knew the moment I gave him my real yes that there was no turning back, and I didn't want to. I spent time with him, stopped listening or watching shows that were ungodly, and went into complete isolation. I'm not saying this will be everyone's process, but this is what I needed to remain focused. I also had a journal where I would express myself to God when I felt like I was going to fall into temptation. I told him every detail of the thoughts that tormented me at nighttime. I would plead with him to deliver me, and as I did this almost every night, I could feel weights being removed from me. I could feel the freedom of God over me. From there, going into regular outside living became easier because I became secured in God. I knew that He was my keeper. I knew that He was my deliverer. I'm sharing this because we as leaders need to understand that we are to help guide God's children, not just our people. People do not belong to us and we cannot treat them as slaves. We can't whip them every time they make a mistake or sell them to another owner when they don't receive the deliverance of God.

We have to ask God to direct us on how to lead those who don't know him and the ones that do. We must understand that because these are His children, He knows them better than we do and yes, we will be disappointed constantly because we have to give our all through the process of helping; but that is our assignment as leaders.

We need to stop treating those who don't look, speak, or walk like us like they don't belong. EVERYONE deserves the reckless love of God. I am a testimony to how God can take someone born into a system of failure and turn her around then user her as a tool for the kingdom. I do not fit at all in the mold the church has created for people to look like. I wear comfortable clothes to church, have big wild hair, and I don't huff and puff when I minister. Instead, I function in the compassion of God. I love those who aren't loved. I shift those that don't want to move. I make those that are comfortable, uncomfortable. God wants us to walk into rooms and cause things to change. He wants us to let him use us. To not be afraid of what people will say when you love the stripper, homeless, or nonbeliever.

God brought to my attention to write this because we are living in a time where God is going to move in radical ways. He caused the church to become uncomfortable within their four walls. Now he is making us go into the world and reach those who were unreachable. You need to be ready to have someone under you that doesn't look anything like you; but they will have the purest love for God. This is the time when the younger generations will rise and reach millions because of their open mindedness. Do not allow religious thinking to stop you from functioning in the fullness of the ministry He entrusted you with.

To those curious to find out more about this radical God that will love you in your unbrokenness, raise your hand and ask Him to show himself to you. He is ready for whatever you throw His way. Come as you are, but get ready to be transformed in His presence. I love you and I ask for your forgiveness if any of us believers have made you feel unwanted or hurt because we didn't understand how to love you. Do not let our actions taint your view of God. He is wonderful, loving, patient, graceful, and merciful.

"Beloved, let us love one another, for love is from God, and whoever loves has been born of God and knows God. Anyone who does not love does not know God, because God is love." (1 John 4:7-8)

To those who have come out of the lifestyle, understand that it will be a process. Some days you will want to look back and return to your old lifestyle, but trust me when I say it won't be worth it. Remain consistent and stay on that narrow road with your vision focused on God, because the time will come where you will be restored and will no longer recognize who you were. If your desire is to be married, then posture yourself before the Lord. I pray that the Lord is with every day and that He will guide your steps. I pray that you may become whole in Him. Trust in God, don't rely on anyone to fulfill you. When my husband came around, I was whole in God. I am now able to teach and bring up my children in a place of Love.

About
Haydee Irving

Haydee Irving affectionately known as an Apostle Haydee is a Minister, CEO, Entrepreneur, Mother, Daughter, Wife and most importantly lover of the King.

She is a bold prophet who walks in the true Apostolic/ Prophetic nature of God never failing to represent Gods true nature.

From a young age Haydee struggled with anger, depression, and anxiety. As a young teenager Haydee was broken and admittedly sought love from alcohol, drugs and homosexual relations. In countless mentions of her testimony Haydee admits she never believed she would make it out of High School alive but, God intervened.

At the tender 19 Haydee encountered and accepted Jesus as Lord and Savior and began to learn more about herself through him.

At the age of 20 Haydee met her husband Prophet Blaine who she later accepted and married in 2017 and together they bore 2 children.

During the 2020 COVID19 pandemic God opened the door to launch her brand new makeup line called Haydee Cosmetics. Her array of shades are long lasting and are each inspired by unique names.

(313) 257-0500 | hello@haydeeirving.com

www.haydeeirving.com

THE LIES HE TOLD

KENYA JOHNSON

The Charmer, Challenger and Con-Artist

He told me he loved me. He said he would never hurt me. I wanted to believe him. I prayed for his words and promises to be true. I dismissed the flaws in his character and gave in to my desperation to feed my emotional needs. It's true, we all have emotional needs, but I wanted that security. I needed to be acknowledged, and I longed to be desired. I allowed my needs to cloud my judgment. My needs drew me closer to him. It was clear that this relationship carried more liabilities than assets. Desperation censored my ability to make sound decisions. I settled, deeming myself unworthy to receive better. I was on a never-ending emotional rollercoaster with no end in sight.

He called me beautiful, and I played the fool, falling for each lie that spewed from his mouth. My self-esteem was on a downward spiral. The images of who I was were collected from the thoughts of others. I turned a blind eye to the warning signs. He was a charmer who challenged my life with the smoothness of a skilled con artist. I became infected by the lies he told. The testimony you are about to read is a brief account of a toxic relationship I had with a man I'll call Mr. Trial. He had characteristics that fit into three categories: The Charmer, the Challenger, and the Con-Artist. Yes, he had all three.

Mr. Trial came into my life during a time when I was vulnerable, an easy prey. I was broken and on my way to recovery, but not yet healed. My self-esteem was low, but slowly building. My relationship with God was on the mend. All I wanted to do was move on, but there was still a part of me that wanted what I saw others have. It was that part of me that fell prey to the charmer, challenger, and the Con-Artist.

The Charmer

I walked into the party feeling confident with the person I was becoming. God was doing a work in me. The healing process had begun. The fragments of my heart my previous relationship had caused were slowly being mended. I had no desire for another relationship. My eyes were focused on God. Mr. Trial introduced himself. He was charming and "easy" on the eyes. The tone of his conversation drew my interest, but the walls around my heart kept me from engaging. His charm was like that of a snake, alluring and almost hypnotizing. The smoothness of his chocolate skin and the deepness of his voice were enticing, to say the least. I told him I was not looking for a relationship, and he led me to believe he only wanted to be friends. We exchanged numbers, and a friendship began.

He wooed me with his talk about his relationship with God. Our friendship progressed. There were things from the beginning that had me skeptical of his truth, but I ignored those thoughts. After all, we were just friends. We continued to talk and eventually started dating. Before I knew it, I was caught up in his charm.

The charmer looks good. He is very appealing to the eye. His demeanor, the way he carries himself, his swag, is what catches your attention. What you are unable to see is his ulterior motives hidden on the inside. The charmer will steal your youth, compromise your integrity, your self-esteem, and your very soul. The snake in the Garden of Eden drew the attention of Eve. His charm swayed her to entertain a conversation. I could just imagine his movements inviting her interest. The deepness of his voice demanding her attention. He was crafty!

"Now the serpent was more crafty (subtle, skilled in deceit) than any living creature of the field which the LORD God had made. And the serpent (Satan) said to the woman, Can it really be that God has said, 'You shall not eat from any tree of the garden'?" And the woman said to the serpent, "We may eat fruit from the trees of the garden, except the fruit from the tree which is in the middle of the garden. God said, 'You shall not eat from it nor touch it; otherwise, you will die.'" (Genesis 3:1-3 AMP)

In my mind, I see Eve as a woman focused on what she knew to be true. She was confident and secure in her identity. She was fearfully and wonderfully made. She knew who she was in God. Yet, the enemy was able to grab her attention. Her focus was broken. The enemy began by asking her a question, giving her the opportunity for a conversation and open dialogue. "Can it really be that God said you shall not eat from any tree of the garden?" It was that question that caused Eve to think twice before she answered.

Have you ever been in a relationship that caused you to second guess what God said or what you knew was true? Even though you may have been seduced by someone skilled in deceit, God is still there to pick up the pieces.

The Challenger

How did I not see it in the beginning? I'm sure the red flags were there. Why was I blinded by the truth that stood before me? Charmers are often characterized as sweet or kindhearted. But in relationships, they are controlling, self-serving, and irresponsible.

Mr. Trial, calculating in his movements, began to break down my defenses. Everything he did was for an underlying purpose. He was clear about his agenda and did his job well. His charm gave the illusion that he was a nice guy. But as time went on, he became controlling and self-centered.

He began attending my church and getting to know my friends and family. He charmed his way into my life and weaved his way into my relationships. Everywhere I went, he was there. We began spending a lot of time together, whether I wanted to or not. In some warped way, we became a couple. My spirit was not at rest, but I was swept up by his charm.

Mr. Trial started his attack against my relationship with God and those I held in high regard. Others could see it, but I couldn't. He began to sow seeds of doubt by questioning those that spoke into my life. His goal was to pull me away from and destroy my support system. He wanted to control me. If my support system was gone, there would be no one to help me see who he really was. Then, he could exercise his control over me with little backlash.

Mr. Trial began to challenge the wisdom of my spiritual leaders. If they said go right, he would give five reasons to go left. He began to challenge my faith in God. If I felt God was leading me a certain way, he would say God told him differently. For every word of wisdom that came my way, he responded with lies disguised as truth. He wanted to be the authority in my life.

The challenger is the one that comes to challenge your faith in God and your identity. He comes armed with lies that sound like the truth to dispute everything God has told You, what you have been taught, and the validity of God's Word. The challenger will twist the truth, lie, distract, accuse, and use irrational and irrelevant arguments if confronted.

"But the serpent said to the woman, 'You certainly will not die!'" (Genesis 3:4 AMP)

The enemy is challenging what God said to Eve. He sowed that seed of doubt, which caused Eve to second guess God. She began to entertain thoughts of doubt – the possibility that God was wrong, and nothing would happen. The enemy challenged what Eve knew to be true. He challenged Eve's relationship with God and her identity in Christ.

The Con Artist

Now I'm caught up. My defenses are down, and Mr. Trial began his con game. He had chipped away at my support system and had my head in a whirlwind. I could not breathe. I was being smothered by his constant presence. He had to know every friend and where I was at all times.

The nature of our relationship progressed, and we became physical. This was a man that claimed salvation; but away from everyone else, he was manipulative. He used the things I told him about my past to hold me to the relationship. He convinced me that he would be the only man who could deal with all my baggage.

I began to give in to what he wanted. I was starting to support him with my finances. I would give him money whenever he needed it. He could never keep a job for more than a few months at a time. My friends began to tell me this relationship was toxic. My family tried to reason with me. People on the outside could see the change in me. Even his own mother told me he was no good.

Nobody will ever love you, but me. Nobody else will ever want you. Your father is trying to control your life. I'm the only man that will ever love you. When I look back, I cringe at the stupid things I did and believed. I felt unworthy of a better relationship.

My prior relationship left wounds that were not healed, and the more pain inflicted on me by Mr. Trial kept those wounds open. They were becoming infected, and it became a race for treatment so I could live the life God designed for me. The con-artist is motivated by greed. He is only interested in what he can get...he is looking for material gain. He knows right from wrong but chooses to do wrong to get what he wants. The con-artist will rob you of your time, energy, and money.

"For God knows that on the day you eat from it your eyes will be opened [that is, you will have greater awareness], and you will be like God, knowing [the difference between] good and evil." And when the woman saw that the tree was good for food, and that it was delightful to look at, and a tree to be desired in order to make one wise and insightful, she took some of its fruit and ate it; and she also gave some to her husband with her, and he ate. (Genesis 3:5-6 AMP)

As the charmer, the enemy gets Eve's attention. As the challenger, he got her to second guess what God had said. He challenged her truth and her identity. Now, the enemy works his con, swindling Eve out of God's best for her life. She was convinced that God had an ulterior motive because Satan, the charmer, challenger, and con-artist broke down her support – her foundation. Eve's faith in God was shaken by Satan's defiance to what God had said. Now she was being swindled into disobeying God.

Eyes Wide Open

I had been charmed, challenged in my faith and identity, and conned. The person I become was unrecognizable. Mr. Trial had taken me for everything. He stripped away my identity. My heart was so overwhelmed with all the things that were going on in my life. My relationship with my parents was distorted. My relationship with God was distorted. I could not find safety in the house of God because this man had come in and infiltrated every area of my life. I began to gain weight and lose my hair. I no longer cared about how I looked. My self-esteem was low. Emotionally I was tattered, battered, and ripped to shreds. Spiritually, I was broken and disconnected. Physically, I was weak. Mentally, I was fragile and no longer confident in my identity.

Mr. Trial now controlled how I saw myself, which gave him access to how I lived. I walked around in a fog of everyday self-medicating to cope. I took Tylenol PM every time I went out with him. I couldn't be with him unless I was out of it. The Tylenol made me sleepy, so I would go in and out when I was with him. I also took muscle relaxers on top of the Tylenol for a condition I had that was triggered by stress. I had to be numb to the things going on around me.

My vision was impaired, and where there is no vision, there is no hope. I once again found myself in a toxic relationship. I allowed him access to my heart. The Bible says,
   "Keep vigilant watch over your heart; that's where life starts." (Proverbs 4:23 MSG)

The desire to be wanted and thought of as beautiful was dictating my actions. I was blinded. When I look back, I can see how my lack of self-esteem caused me to make a lot of wrong choices. My parents and grandparents were praying for me. They prayed that my eyes would be opened to see Mr. Trial for what he was. I have to admit, I knew this relationship was toxic but the nature of our relationship caused soul ties.

We were linked together, tied at the soul. I had become entangled. No matter how bad I wanted to be free, I couldn't get him out of my life. We had become intimate, and that intimacy tied us together in ways that wouldn't allow me the freedom I needed. My world was consumed with the relationship. Mr. Trial wouldn't allow me to breathe my own air. Everywhere I went, he would be there. It was difficult getting away from him. He wanted to control where I went and what I did. He would even drive me to class and wait outside the door until I was done.

My parents tried everything they could to get me away from him. They refused to allow him in our home but that didn't stop me from seeing him; after all, I was grown up. I moved in with my grandparents because of the back and forth with my parents regarding Mr. Trial. I would tell myself every day to break up with him; I would even practice it. The days I felt strongly about it, he would do something that caused me to doubt what I knew was the right thing to do. On Valentine's day, my father sent me a dozen roses and a card where he asked me to dinner. I was reluctant to accept because I knew the conversation would be about Mr. Trial, but I agreed. He took me to one of my favorite restaurants where we tried to sit and have a pleasant dinner. I had already decided I was going to stand my ground and not allow my father to tell me what I should and should not do. We made small talk, but the tension between us was almost unbearable. Finally, my father just blurted out, "Are you going to marry Mr. Trial or what?"

The very nature of his question brought down my defenses. I had always said that if my father could not walk me down the aisle and give me away, then that guy wasn't worth it. I knew in my heart that my father would not give me away to Mr. Trial. I could see the concern and hurt in my father's eyes as he revealed to me what he had learned about Mr. Trial from his former pastor. Not only was Mr. Trial trying to control my life, he was still stalking his ex-girlfriend by going to her job and hiding behind bushes. It was that night that I decided to leave the relationship. I knew I had to walk away, but it wasn't going to be easy. My eyes were open to the state I was in.

Then the eyes of the two of them were opened [that is, their awareness increased], and they knew that they were naked, and they fastened fig leaves together and made themselves coverings. (Genesis 3:7 AMP)

Eve had a similar experience. The enemy had deceived her. His charm intrigued her. He challenged her faith and identity in God. He conned her into believing and acting on a lie. It wasn't until all of this took place that her eyes were opened. She was aware that she had been deceived. She could see clearly that her life would forever be changed.

Breaking Free

What made me go back to him over and over again? Was it desperation? Maybe. Did I fear the repercussions? Yes, but I knew the relationship needed to end. Truth is, I feared what would happen if I did. He knew too many secrets, and he threatened to tell. He wanted to hold me to the relationship. He wanted to control me. He did not love me, but he didn't want to give another man a chance either. He, through my embarrassment, chased away all my friends – male and female. I wanted to reach out for help. I prayed for someone to see me, I mean truly see me and rescue me from this awful place.

I had shamed my family name. I did things I wasn't proud of by allowing this man to manipulate me. I was deceived into believing things would get better after listening to his all too frequent tearful pleadings for forgiveness. I was a mentally battered woman looking into the eyes of her abuser, begging me to stay. He didn't want to be alone. He didn't want the best thing that happened to him to leave; but he didn't want me, the woman that cared for and supported him.

Mr. Trial had embarrassed me before, and it was difficult to recover from the things he did. If I did something he disliked, I was yelled at, forced to endure public embarrassment, or be subject to his verbal humiliation. I know you must be thinking, "Who would allow someone to treat them this way?" Looking back now, I wonder that same thing. But when you have identity issues, these things can easily take place.

In our scripture reference, we see that Eve had no issues with her identity until the enemy planted a seed of doubt in her mind. The seed continued to grow, until eventually she allowed it to take over and control her actions. Now she is naked, vulnerable, and exposed to the things of the world and susceptible to its folly.

Freedom comes at a cost. For us to be free, the Father had to give His only son to be ridiculed, embarrassed, talked about, and be physically, mentally, and verbally abused. He was falsely accused and sentenced to death as everyone watched, just for us to be free.

I had a decision to make. I wanted to be free, but it was going to cost me. My secrets would be told. I would be hunted and sought out by him in his efforts to regain control. Mr. Trial knew the relationship was coming to an end. He had hoped getting me pregnant would help him keep control. I can't say it was all his fault because I allowed it.

I once again stepped into his trap. After my decision to leave my toxic relationship, I started talking to a male friend, Brian. Brian had pursued me twice. He was a young preacher who loved God with his whole heart. I was emotionally vulnerable but guarded. I had become hard and began putting up walls to protect my heart. I did not want to hurt any longer. I no longer wanted to feel the pain or deal with the stress. These walls I built kept me safe from the outside world, but they also held me captive to the pain I inflicted on myself.

Brian came into my life equipped with everything he needed to break down those walls. He had heard from God and came with a plan. He began pursuing me again - this time with careful intent. Everything he did was intentional with no underlying agenda other than to love me – baggage and all. There was something different about this man. Something I had never experienced before. I began enjoying his company and conversation.

It had only been a few weeks after breaking things off with Mr. Trial. I was not ready for another relationship, but I was open to a friendship. At this time, Brian lived an hour away. We talked almost every day and would occasionally see each other on the weekend. The distance between us helped me keep things in perspective. There was no pressure, just friendly conversation.

A month after my break-up and a month into my new friendship with Brian, I found out that I was pregnant. This was a devastating blow. It was like Mr. Trial had again entered my life to control the outcome. Not only was there a soul tie, this child would forever bind us together. My actions following my discovery were calculating and intentional.

Terminating my pregnancy was the most difficult decision I had ever made. My decision for doing so may anger some, and I won't try to justify my actions. I chose what I felt was best at the time and, in turn, I suffered the consequences of my actions. Depression set in and the mental anguish began. I tried to push Brian away. He didn't deserve a woman so broken and battered. He didn't deserve to be treated out of my pain.

Learning to Love Again

Brian was not going to allow me to walk away from our friendship without a fight. He did not know there was already an inward battle taking place. He didn't push me to reveal what was going on within; he just kept his presence known. He would leave roses and small gifts on my doorstep whenever I refused to talk. He would write me poems and cards to let me know he was thinking about me. He would take me for dessert and quiet walks by the water. I did not have to say a word. He let me know that just being there was enough.

Before you can learn to love another, you must learn to love yourself. You have to love the person God made you to be and make no excuses for it. From an early age, I had self-esteem issues. As a child, I took every negative word spoken over me to heart. I lived and longed for my father's approval. Any word of disapproval would send me spiraling into a ball of emotional turmoil. I'm sure my father was unaware of how his less than encouraging words affected me. I never doubted my father's love for me; but his quest to be a strong male figure in my life left room for the enemy to attack.

I spent years trying to win his approval. Every time he looked at me, I thought he was seeing me through every negative word spoken. This followed me through every relationship.

I searched for the approval of men. I even felt my relationship with the Heavenly Father was contingent on His approval of me. I had to realize that I needed to heal. I had wounds that had been opened for years. Each bad choice and toxic relationship infected those wounds.

I had to learn to love the "me" God made. I had to understand that I didn't have to be perfect or live a perfect life, and it was okay to make mistakes. Each mistake didn't put a target on my back for a life of disappointment. I learned to take each mistake as an opportunity to get better.

I learned to squash every negative word spoken to me and over me with the Word of God. Prayers went up for me, and I began to heal. Brian came along just in time to pour into me. I could be open and honest, no matter how crazy my thoughts were. My self-esteem began to build.

The Holy Spirit used Brian to minister to me. His eyes were opened to being able to truly see me. I began seeing myself differently. The fragmented pieces of my life were being gathered as our relationship progressed. I learned to live again by allowing God to orchestrate my relationships. I learned to love again by not conforming to other's opinions of me. I learned to love again by seeing myself through the eyes of God and not through the eyes of man.

No matter what you've done, God is always there to pick up the pieces of your life. If you allow Him to rule and reign in your life, He will guide you to the right relationship in His timing. Take note of the following lessons I've learned:

1. Submit your relationship to God and allow Him to open your eyes to the things around you. Recognizing that your relationship is toxic is the first step. Allow the Holy Spirit to bring light into the relationship and open your eyes to see it for what it is.

2. If you're in a toxic relationship, ask the Father to help you break free from the ties that bind you. Breaking free can be difficult. Soul ties or the things that bind you to a relationship can be strong. It's often the very thing that keeps you there or causes you to return after walking away.

Allow the Father to gather the fragmented pieces of your heart so you can learn to love again. After breaking free, give every piece of your heart to the Father and allow Him to put them back together. Let Him pour into you and show you what real love looks like. When you do these things, you will learn to love again.

About Kenya Johnson

Kenya Johnson is a certified life coach and owner of the Total Makeover Company, where her motto is "Activating and Building the Woman in You." She has a passion for writing and has authored various books on relationships and self-esteem building. Kenya lives in Michigan with her husband (Brian) of twenty-three years and three children, Brian II (21), Brandon (17), and Jocelyn (12).

(313) 740-7059 | kenya0804@aol.com
www.thetotalmakeover.com

WHAT'S LOVE GOT TO DO WITH IT

TIFFANY PATTON

Misguided love.

Tina Turner sings the song, *What's love got to do, got to do with it?* I never realized that would be the theme song for my life, nor that it would be the trillion-dollar question that, if answered correctly, my life would have possibly taken a different turn. What I did not realize is that love has everything to do with the things I would encounter and endure. You see, there are different types of love, and I have encountered a few. The lack of it or abundance of it can desperately change the outcome of any person. Most importantly, misguided love will and can destroy most people. At least that is what it's purposed to do.

As far back as I could remember, love has always been a thing I was drawn to. I was the only 5-year-old that I knew of in love with the likes of Doris Day movies, Fred Astaire, and the like. Yes, I enjoyed the dancing and singing (being a lover of the arts even at that tender age), but the main thing that drew me to the cinematography was the appearance and interaction of love! Who does this at 5? I'm not sure why or when it became something that I not only thought about and talked about but acted out. Even at the age of 6, I was talking as Barbie and Ken of marriage, etc.

Maybe it was because I watched the love my parents had for one another (married 32 years-wow) and desired the same. Or maybe it was the fact that, at that very same age of 6, my life would forever be changed, and I used them to escape from my new reality.

At age 6, I, unfortunately, began being molested by not just one of my cousins but two. Yes, the horrid events I had to endure were something a 6-year-old should not have to endure. You would think that having that tragic 6-year span event (oh yeah forgot to mention I stopped being molested when my one cousin found out that I received my menstrual-I guess he figured he would get caught if I came up pregnant), so even my abusers discarded me. One would think that love at this point would be skewed in some sense because the same two people who were supposed to love me and protect me violated me. But they were supposed to love me, right?

One would think that after such an ordeal that dealing with a boy or even wanting a relationship would be the last thing anyone would desire. However, it was contrary to me. I still had crushes etc. I think the desire to be loved intensified after that, not in a fast or perverted way, but in the purest form. I just wanted to be loved.

Fast forward 13 years, and I found myself in love for the second time. Yes well, the first time ended devastatingly, but I, unfortunately, fell in love with the wrong one. I was 18 and had lost my first love to a murder at the age of 16, but we will not discuss that right now; that is another story for another time. The second love of my life, the one who helped me get over the first. Yep, that's right, most people of sound mind and clarity see this as a disaster waiting to happen because he would be the rebound guy. However, it wasn't like that. I knew him before my "first" love, and if truth be told, I liked him first. At the age of 19, I became pregnant with our daughter, and out of the blue with no conversation or discussion, "our" became "mines!" He wasn't there for most of the pregnancy. Talk about rejection on another
level.

I did not even bother calling him when I went into labor. But I asked my best friend once she was born, and he said that he would be there for us. We became a couple, a problematic couple. See, I was the one that had a place, car, etc. I motivated him and encouraged him to begin his business, etc. It was going so well that we moved in together, and "he" was talking marriage. He even asked me to marry him. I said yes, Oh, I'm sorry, did I fail to mention with no ring. I would faithfully awaken at 5 am and pray, I did not even know that this was something you were supposed to do. I just was led to do it. See, in the beginning, I also fell headfirst for God at the age of 6. I attended GOD'S WAY church down the street where my cousin Herbert Ross was the pastor, Sunday school, and all. I loved to attend; however, there was a part of the service normally towards the end where what I called, "the part where people started dying," that I would run out of the church and run the two blocks all the way home, scared and not understanding what was being seen, and swore I wasn't going back. Lol, yeah, I guess somewhere in there I understood that these people were not dying because they would be there the next Sunday, but I regress.

The purpose of my saying that was to state that I have always had a relationship with God, and the most beautiful part about it was it was never pressed upon me. Not that my parents were heathens, they simply worked most Sundays, and my interest and love of God came from Him. But one day, I found that he had gotten his ex-pregnant while we were living together, and she was due within a few months. When my child's father decided not to be a part or be lukewarm as a father,

I knew who I could lean on, and God overall would assist and help me raise this beautiful bundle of joy. Even if he didn't realize it, she was a gift! See, this rejection and betrayal didn't just hurt me, I began to see how the hurt had affected my daughter, and in time I would find this out in a major way (for another story). After several broken promises, cheating, and simply not being a father to my daughter, I decided to move on completely. Now, remember, this was the "friend" I had known well before she was born. Again, misguided love had injured me once again, but this time I didn't care because of me; it was seeing how that same misguided love had now hurt my daughter. Well, I took the fragments left behind from the third time I was mishandled and focused on God,

My daughter, school, and church! Yes, the zeal I had for Jesus was on 100K! there is no way to run into misguided love with God, right?! I became a member of a church where I desired to serve and raise my daughter.

I wanted her to know that, with God we would and shall overcome. There wasn't anything that God couldn't do or handle. There wasn't anything I wouldn't do for HIM. So, anything I was asked to do in "church," I did. I was part of a dance ministry that I loved. It was over a dance group that I was scared straight to do with the kids my daughter's age when asked (but surprisingly enough, God revealed something about myself I didn't know I had within). I was in ministerial classes, I drove the church van every Sunday, and sometimes Wednesdays for bible study. I was in the praise and worship team, and I was my Bishop's secretary, you name it I did it. I was all things for all people for about eight years. Oh, did I mention I lost my mother to breast cancer during this time?

My routine set, my daughter, church, work, school, church, and all over again. Then, I was wounded badly within the church. Yet, another story for another time, but I clearly remember praying one morning when the Holy Spirit said to me, "You've been affected, NOW move before you become infected!" I was so scared, audibly hearing God. I obeyed immediately and never went back! After just a few days of not going to church, not knowing where to go, and my car being down, I called a friend crying and told him the story.

A few days later, my daughter and I were introduced and taken to another church. One I would see was ordained for me to be at. I kept very focused as the years went on, but my life began feeling so empty and void of SOOO much, yet safe! I had been celibate for almost seven years and still daughter, church, work, and home. Until that day the world stood still. There he was captivating in stature and conversation.

There was a fire that ignited within me something I think I had forgotten even existed. We began talking on the phone daily, almost all night, and no matter how much I tried to just stay phone pals, he insisted that we meet. I ignored it, of course. But then one day, he showed up to an event and everything changed.

I found myself in this whirlwind relationship that, if I am completely honest, was with a man who I honestly, completely, and wholeheartedly respected and fell in love with. Sincerely! But see, there was one thing that made this dream fairytale relationship into a nightmare. He was married! Yes, I said it. Married. Now do not get me wrong, it wasn't the normal marriage relationship that one would think. He was separated but still married.

This is why I truly believed that the "prophetic words" I had received from several individuals were true. I was told, "that is your husband." I remember saying to one, "but you don't understand." They then said, "oh, why, because he is married? God showed me that, even though I didn't know. That is still your husband, continue to pray and allow God to do the rest." I was given scriptures and all. I understand you are now probably saying this girl must have been slow! And who are these people who helped her go deeper into the abyss of hell? Well, no, I was not slow, just misguided. You see, the love I received early on in my life from the very beginning were misguided.

From the perverted love of my cousins, then the love I received that was brutally taken away, to the misguided love from someone who should have covered my daughter and me but chose to walk away. All this inevitably led me to slowly but surely loose myself somehow. You seem sin causes destruction, but because the enemy strategizes and will wait you out, he allows you to kill and destroy yourself slowly but surely. You see, the truth of the matter is, this was not about the married man, it was about me. Crazier to say, this relationship was necessary for my life. Now, how can she say that you're probably thinking? Well, because this was what it took to reveal the lies of the enemy and the strategies the enemy had been using over my entire life to steal, kill, and destroy me. And it was also what pushed me to the end of myself.

You see, all my misguided love relationships are what caused me to come to the end of myself. This last relationship I loved him with my total being. I can say I believed I loved him as a wife should love her husband, but the truth is I loved him despite myself. One day – I finally realized I was waiting for yet another person to love me and choose me, waiting on another person to see my value and see my heart. I was waiting to love another and finally get the overall commitment from someone who clearly was not capable of giving it. It was never that I was treated as a "side piece," because I wasn't a secret, which is why I truly thought this was my husband. I was told that God never told him to marry her, but he did so because of what he was going through at the time. But see, ladies, I had come to a point where I was tired! Tired of it all! Tired of yet another person failing to see that the most beautiful parts lay within, failing to see the value that I thought I had made plain to see.

I remember calling him to try and resolve a misunderstanding. It's easy to be played when the other person knows that you don't really value yourself and want to deal with fear and rejection. At that very moment, I just became disgusted with myself! I had enough but I didn't know what to do. I then heard the Holy Spirit say, "Baby girl, you are desiring someone to see the value that you haven't allowed yourself to see." I remember crying so hard and saying, "God I'm SOOO tired of this relationship, I'm not happy.

My happiness is temporary, and what I truly want and deserve is not showing up. Love cannot be this hard!" Then I heard, LOVE is not this hard! I then began to cry and say, "God I want to walk away, but this is SOOO hard because I love him soooooo much!" Then I said the words, "God, please help me to walk away- I can't do this by myself, please help me!" I then heard God say, who do you love more?

Unconditional Love of the Father

At that very moment tears belted out of me as I said, "YOU LORD! I don't want anything without you, I'm scared to lose you more. So, Father give me the strength to walk away from him, I love him so much, but this thing has unknowingly stripped me of myself." I cried myself to sleep, and when I awoke, there was a strength that I cannot even explain. From that day to this, I never called, texted, or saw him again. I was intentional. He would be my "last misguided love."

You see, the person designed for you never has to be shown who you are because it is evident. What is most important is that you know who you are first. As the days, weeks and months went on, God began showing me who I was in HIM. It began two weeks after surrendering the ungodly relationship to God. I decided to be re-baptized. I wanted to start again and restore myself unto God and cleanse myself of all unrighteousness as in John 1:9. What was most important for me to do was to not backslide nor allow the enemies or whispering spirits to cause me to look back. Now, what's funny is that my desire to surrender all to God and seek him like never before and healing had become my only desire.

What became apparent to me over a short period is that I had given away way too much of myself. Not just in the last relationship, but over time. God took me through a series of thoughts and showed me many areas of my life that I had not healed from and needed to!

You see, I never took the time to heal from being molested by two family members. Even though at two different times I told my family, I never felt as if anyone fought for me.

My mother was ashamed and embarrassed, I'm sure, due to it being her family. And then my Father, the one who, once I finally informed him (mind you I was grown when I did), I thought would somehow just affirm me. I was not mad at him or even blamed him. I loved my dad and understood that he was working and did not have a clue. I honestly didn't become broken by him until it was clear that he didn't believe me.

One day as I was trying to explain to my daughter why I'm so weird about her staying over at others' houses and what I went through so she would understand; my father asked me to stop lying to her! That turned into a situation that caused us to have an estranged relationship for a moment. Then, losing my first love to death, oh sidebar, I forgot to mention that I dreamed about what happened six months before it happened and just as I dreamed it is how it happened. I have witnesses to who I told the dream to who were floored when it happened, this again is another story for another time.

Then, being rejected by my child's father, and what I believe hurt me most was not that I was rejected, but that he rejected MY daughter! Then there was the loss of my mother (oh, that was another lesson) to cancer. Whew! I just felt like one thing after the other was coming at me, where I just kept getting up and shaking myself off and believing God while being positive and being the "strong one." Does that sound familiar to you? You have to understand that to truly be strong and present for others and able to be what others need you to be, wife, husband, sister, friend, counselor, minister, pastor, daughter, or son; you must first put on the oxygen mask and make sure you are ok by loving yourself. But we cannot get there until we can forgive ourselves and then see what God says about you. He says that you are wonderfully and beautifully made. It states that "*In Him, you have been made Complete (achieving spiritual stature through Christ*" (Colossians 2:10, AMP).

Just to name a few, there were many things he had to show me, which only came from staying in the Word of God and spending time with Him. He replaced all the countless times I spent in the wrong relationship with spending time with him. And it wasn't always pretty, sometimes they were ugly. Some days and nights, I had to cry because of my flesh. The separating and severing of soul ties hurt because I had become familiar and shared my life with someone. You see, when a soul tie is broken, think about it like this. If, when you are married, the two become one. Think about when you consummate your marriage, you are doing the same thing even if you are not married. Whoever you become connected with (which doesn't always have to be sexual. It can be with a friend, etc.) someone on a deeper level, it's where a soul tie happens.

You are not only connected to that person, but spiritually, you are now connected to everyone they have been intimate with as well. "*What good will it be for someone to gain the whole world, yet forfeit their soul? Or what can anyone give in exchange for their soul?*" (Matthew 16:26)

Soul ties must be broken, and deliverance can only come from God. The more time I spent with God, the stronger I felt, and what's amazing is even though I had no clue as to where I lost myself, God was able to take me to that exact place. You see, what I really needed all these years wasn't a man or a relationship with one, but a true and real relationship with God. Remember, my routine was daughter, work, church, and sometimes school. Most people think that works within the four walls equate to a relationship.

Although, I had a relationship with God, it surfaced due to my zeal. I allowed works and pleasing those around me within and outside of the church doing good works substitute my time needed with God. But what I really needed to have done was focus on my relationship and intimacy with Him. That is where I found peace, love and joy, and true restoration. Then I found the key to walking a life of purpose. The life that God intended for me. That key was the unconditional love of the Father. I began to meditate on scriptures like Jeremiah 31:3, which says, "*I have loved you with an everlasting love*," and Leviticus 26:11. "*Moreover, I will make MY dwelling among you, and MY soul will NOT reject you!*"

Self-love Restored

Most people see and understand self-love as an outward expression or action. We usually think of self-love as a day at the spa, going on a shopping spree, or treating yourself to dinner or lunch. On the contrary, those are things or byproducts of "true" self-love. True self-love is understanding who you are in Christ through the eyes and mind of God, knowing who he says you are. The more I studied (growth is an ongoing process), the more revelation I am given as to not only who I am but the authority I possess. You see, there is not any area of your life that you will be able to master or thrive within when you are broken. When you struggle with not knowing your value and worth (the difference between knowing and understanding), you can mistakenly allow others to make deductions and withdrawals that they should not have access to be even able to take. When left unhealed, you are likened to someone who is hemorrhaging, and where the internal bleeding began is not where it remains. When you bleed enough, it begins to spill over into other organs, other areas of your life. By the time you look up you will have wondered how your life got in such a mess, but it's because you are hemorrhaging.

What you do not realize is that it isn't just that your life is a mess, it's that you are slowly dying. The enemy will wait YOU out. He comes to steal, kill, and destroy. But once you have come to the revelation of who you are, as I did; you will find that self-love is not what people paint it to be. It is not selfish to focus on the healing of oneself. In seeking God with all fervency, I found ME! The person I had lost, I found. The revelation that God showed me -catch this- is that I was never lost. I WAS THERE ALL ALONG. HOWEVER, I HAD BEEN BURIED UNDER ALL THE DIRTY AND UNCLEAN GARMENTS, EXPECTATIONS AND MASKS THE VARIOUS PEOPLE DESIRE AND EXPECT OF ME. Because I did not fully know who I was in Christ, I tried to be who others needed me to be when it was convenient for them. The unconditional love of the Father freed me from my self-defeating actions, but it also delivered me from the approval of others.

True self-love is walking in the fullness and freedom of who God designed you to be, unapologetically. In Him, no approval is needed because you understand that you have been stamped "Approved by God even before you were yet in your mother's womb." If you live for the acceptance of others, you will die from their rejection! It is at the end of yourself where you find yourself.

When your sense of self-worth is based on the approval of others, your value is at the mercy of what these others think about you. Your identity in who you are and how you view yourself is now determined by how others see you. Now I understand why God kept singing to me, "What's love got to do, got to do with it???" Just as Tina Turner endured many tragedies and heartaches, desiring to be loved and accepted, her fear of rejection caused her to position herself to being misused and abused. This caused her to be in relationships that she was too valuable to place herself within. She gave her control and power over to another human being, someone who wasn't authorized nor qualified to have it. Only God is allowed to have control over our lives. Relinquishing our fear of rejection over to God and being genuinely transparent with him regarding my hurts, I then had to allow his unconditional love to saturate me until I was ready to trust God enough to be able to exchange my fear for faith, which is where I found my full acceptance in the hands of God. It was then that I accepted his love for myself, knowing my worth, and establishing boundaries and standards. It was with me as it was with Tina Turner in the biopic. What's love got to do with it? It was at the end of myself. This is where I came to myself and was able to stand strong in who God created me to be. Unapologetically.

About
Tiffany Patton

Media is a way of life for Native Detroiter, Tiffany Patton. With an enduring passion for media and empowering others in tow, Tiffany is often recognized as a modern-day renaissance woman. In May 2011, Tiffany sought to premiere the first radio broadcast of On the Go with Tiffany Patton. The Detroit based radio show gained much traction and became the source of neo soul, jazz, soul & gospel music. From thought provoking topics, interviews and engaging conversations with guest celebrity hosts, artists and public and political personalities, the show evolved into a TV show that exudes the same excitement as the radio show & later a successful podcast heard on IHeartradio, Spotify, Itunes, Amazon, etc. This podcast then began a successful video podcast seen weekly on YouTube.

This media maven covers media in all avenues from television, radio and now print as she has been a contributing writer for national magazine Hope for Women Magazine & Impact Atlanta Magazine and recently became the Editor in Chief of Impact Detroit International Magazine as well. She is the owner & founder of Enerlight Candle Co. & just recently launched her Hair & Beauty line Crowned Glorious Hair & Beauty which is a subsidiary of her company Crowned Glorious. Mother of a very beautiful and talented daughter to boot. In 2018, she added author to her as she was the coauthor of Push Through-How the Process leads you to the Promise. Among her accomplishments as an entrepreneur and philanthropist, Tiffany is a recipient of the Spirit of Detroit Award (2017). Tiffany was also just recently featured in Rolling Out Magazines business column as the "Emerging Player in the Media Industry". She was also honored by Native Detroit Magazine in of November 2017 for her contributions to media and entrepreneurship. Ms. Tiffany Patton lastly doesn't take lightly being that of a minister & life coach as her serving and helping others holds dearest to her heart. Tiffany Patton uses her influence & national platform to uplift, encourage, empower and inspire all she encounters, in short Ms. Patton exemplifies a modern-day renaissance woman.

Instagram: onthegotp | Facebook: Tiffany Patton Trillionairess
Twitter: @TiffanyNPatton | LinkedIn: Tiffany Patton

(313) 740-7059 | tiffanypatton@gmail.com
www.onthegowithtiffanypatton.com

BROKEN INTO GREATNESS

Lakina Fulks

There is beauty in brokenness

I spent years thinking I was whole, but it was a wholeness that was fragile and built by the hands of men. I was like a document left in the rain. Untouched and in a puddle it appeared whole, but if you retrieved it from the water without care, it would start to tear, and as you moved it, the words would begin fading away until the fragile document becomes as soft as tissue paper. Careful, it may disintegrate. I was soft as tissue paper, but I thought I was unbreakable. Molested at a very early age, married multiple times, and enduring some of the hardest times that most women my age never experienced or could even imagine. And I was still standing. So, I had to be unbreakable. Right?

Little did I know that everything I would go through was preparing me for my destiny, and I do mean everything. As a young girl, I was molested by a close relative. He not only molested me but my sister as well. At first, I was always the one he came after. As my sister started getting older, he started abusing her too. But being her big sister, I would do anything to protect her, including accepting the abuse meant for her so she would not have to go through it. This went on for years, to the point that I learned to just accept it when it happened. My sister wanted to tell what was happening to us, but I didn't want anyone to be upset with our abuser, and I definitely didn't want to be accused of lying. I learned to be silent and taught my sister the same. And soon, I came to believe silence was a strength. Although I was a child and suffering from something so horrible, I thought that so long as no one knew, I had power. I was learning to have control. That control would soon take me into darker places. Broken by the hands of men, not yet molded into the image of God.

My first and second marriage were both complicated. My first was a world of domestic abuse and disrespect. My second marriage brought me a husband that had a drug addiction. In both marriages I was silent about the things I was suffering from because presenting myself as perfect to everyone meant I still had control, and I was unbreakable. Throughout these years, I obtained multiple college degrees and started a real estate company, all while raising six children. I was going through hell, but you had to be very close to me to truly know what was happening in my life. Even those closest to me never really understood the details of what was happening, because again, I taught myself to be silent and always look perfect. Always say the right things. Cover up the black eyes. Never show mental weakness. Keep a beautiful smile on your face. Remain loyal to the abusers. Broken by the hands of men, not yet molded into the image of God.

It wasn't until I lost a child that I could no longer uphold the façade of being perfect and strong. This occurred during a very stressful and tumultuous time of my second marriage. My second husband was actually a wonderful person, but his drug addiction made him unbearable and irresponsible as a husband and a father. Despite prayer and having faith, I lost my son, my seventh child. My husband said it happened because I did not pray hard enough, but I believed it was his drug use that was too much for our baby to survive. We were both hurting, but my husband could not be there for me. Drugs were his comfort, and I was left to myself with that familiar loneliness that was my constant companion my whole life. It was the loneliness of pain and suffering. The loneliness of always appearing perfect. The loneliness of pushing others out so they could not see the turmoil. The loneliness of silence. But now, it was too much, and the silence was deafening. All my issues and hurt were spilling out for all to see. Broken by the hands of men, not yet molded into the image of God. *My [only] sacrifice [acceptable] to God is a broken spirit; A broken and contrite heart [broken with sorrow for sin, thoroughly penitent], such, O God, You will not despise.* (Psalm 51:17 AMP)

And just like King David, I had come to my end. After losing my baby boy, my second marriage soon ended. I was now a single mom, living on my own with six children. At first it felt odd doing everything on my own, until I came to the realization that I had been by myself for years. Married but single. I had been married twice but never experienced a relationship where I was truly partnered with anyone. It was at that point God began to deal with me, and He was able to show me where I had been living in sin for years. That's right, me. The one broken by the hands of men. The abuse I had suffered from men was obviously wrong. It seemed like I had been asking God my entire life why He allowed others to abuse and hurt me. He was the Almighty God. I believed the Bible and what it said about everything He was and what He was capable of doing. I told Him, "But yet, you allowed me to suffer so much abuse. And now, at this moment, you were talking to me about where I was wrong. Me?" I was broken by the hands of men. But God responded that I was not yet molded into His image.

What did being molded into His image mean? I had given my life to Him as a child. I was a prayer warrior, minister, and ready to tell the world about His goodness. But how could I truly recognize how good he was if I could not appreciate the beauty of his creation in me. It had been easy for me to testify about what he had done for me outwardly. I never died from the hands of abuse. Despite my second husband's drug problems, God always took care of my children and me. He helped me survive depression, and I still succeeded in life; but the truth behind it all was that I did not feel worthy of any of it. And right in that, He showed me the unworthiness I had carried for years was the sin that so easily beset me.

GATHERING THE FRAGMENTS

The First Stage: The Egg

Let's consider the process of a butterfly. According to butterflysite.com:

All butterflies have "complete metamorphosis." To grow into an adult, they go through 4 stages: egg, larva, pupa, and adult. Each stage has a different goal...Depending on the type of butterfly, the life cycle of a butterfly may take anywhere from one month to a whole year.

A butterfly starts life as a tiny, round, oval, or cylindrical egg. The coolest thing about butterfly eggs, especially monarch butterfly eggs, is that if you look close enough, you can actually see the tiny caterpillar growing inside of it. Some butterfly eggs may be round, some oval, and some may be ribbed while others may have other features. The egg shape depends on the type of butterfly that laid the egg.

Psalm 139:13-16 (ESV) states, *"For you formed my inward parts; you knitted me together in my mother's womb. I praise you, for I am fearfully and wonderfully made."*

Just like the egg for the caterpillar, a woman's womb is the place of our beginnings; the place where we are uniquely made, unlike anyone else. We have no form or shape, but God already sees who we are. From the very start of our life, He can already see the end. He makes no mistakes. Your entry into the world was masterfully planned despite all the circumstances that occur outside of the womb. Zechariah 4:10 says, *"Do not despise these small beginnings, for the LORD rejoices to see the work begin..."* God has a plan for every stage of our lives.

The Second Stage: The Larva

Butterflysite.com describes the second stage of the butterfly as:

When the egg finally hatches, most of you would expect for a butterfly to emerge, right? Well, not exactly. In the butterfly's life cycle, there are four stages, and this is only the second stage. Butterfly larvae are actually what we call caterpillars. Caterpillars do not stay in this stage for very long, and mostly, in this stage, all they do is eat.

When the egg hatches, the caterpillar will start his work and eat the leaf they were born onto. This is important because the mother butterfly needs to lay her eggs on the type of leaf the caterpillar will eat – each caterpillar type likes only certain types of leaves. Since they are tiny and cannot travel to a new plant, the caterpillar needs to hatch on the kind of leaf it wants to eat.

Once a child is born, depending on their parents or situations, they become part of an environment that will shape their lives. Some of us will look back at our childhoods and attest that we had a wonderful upbringing, while for others the testimony is quite the opposite. Regardless, both environments are essential for shaping that particular child. Just like the mother butterfly, God already knows what type of environment we will be placed in. Some are made of security and love; others are filled with pain and rejection. But we need to remember the importance of the first stage of the butterfly. Each egg is filled with a caterpillar unique to what type of butterfly it will become, just as God knows exactly what type of being, He created for the world. The painful environment is just as important as the one filled with love. If you are in the middle of your process while reading this, you might think it seems selfish of God; but like the caterpillar, we must eat from this specific environment because there is a future you that needs a certain "leaf" or "life" to withstand the journey.

The Third Stage: Pupa (Chrysalis)

The caterpillar emerges and eats from the leaf where it was hatched. Butterflysite.com gives us more insight into the third stage of the butterfly; the pupa:

The pupa stage is one of the coolest stages of a butterfly's life. As soon as a caterpillar is done growing and they have reached their full length/weight, they form themselves into a pupa, also known as a chrysalis. From the outside of the pupa, it looks as if the caterpillar may just be resting, but the inside is where all the action is. Inside the pupa, the caterpillar is rapidly changing.

Now, as most people know, caterpillars are short, stubby, and have no wings at all. Within the chrysalis, the old body parts of the caterpillar are undergoing a remarkable transformation, called 'metamorphosis,' to become the beautiful parts that make up the butterfly that will emerge. Tissue, limbs, and organs of a caterpillar have all been changed by the time the pupa is finished and is now ready for the final stage of a butterfly's life cycle.

For many of us, life is challenging; filled with lows and highs, most of them unexpected. Some of the challenges we bring upon ourselves. The effects of these problems are sometimes the hardest because these are the issues the Enemy or our consciousness loves to remind us of what we did; sometimes sending you through years of guilt and self-loathing. But like that caterpillar in its third stage of change, it forms into a Pupa; chrysalis and begins an inner work of change. God invites us into His rest to be born...again.

Once we give our lives to God and allow Him to start working within us, we begin to change inside, just like the caterpillar. A remarkable transformation happens, and the years of hurt, pain, anguish, misunderstandings, and confusion are put to rest by accepting Jesus as our Lord and Savior. Like the caterpillar in its chrysalis, you cannot see an immediate change because you are still being formed. This is the stage where the Enemy usually tries to abort the process and remind you of what you were before you surrendered to God. But you must remain in the process, the chrysalis, until God is finished with His work.

The Fourth Stage: Adult Butterfly

There is always a process that we remain in, in Christ, so long as we are still in the earth. But there does come a time when God allows us to see that a maturity has taken place inside of us, and the work He has done on us is manifested. Butterflysite.com gives us insight on the last stage of the butterfly:

Finally, when the caterpillar has done all its forming and changing inside the pupa if you are lucky, you will get to see an adult butterfly emerge. When the butterfly first emerges from the chrysalis, both wings are going to be soft and folded against its body.

This is because the butterfly had to fit all its new parts inside of the pupa.

As soon as the butterfly has rested after coming out of the chrysalis, it will pump blood into the wings to get them working and flapping – then they get to fly. Usually, within a three or four-hour period, the butterfly will master flying and will search for a mate in order to reproduce.

When in the fourth and final stage of their lives, adult butterflies are constantly on the lookout to reproduce, and when a female lays their eggs on some leaves, the butterfly life cycle will start all over.

God allows us to go through many obstacles in life. Some of our troubles even start in the womb. But being the creator of all things, He sees the end in the beginning and knows that this baby in the womb will one day become a fully striving adult who will work His purpose in the earth. And when you allow Him to do the inner work and mature you by allowing His thoughts to guide us, spiritual fruit begins to manifest in excellent works and we become trees that others can pick from. We are now ready to fly among this world; conquering and dominating with purpose in any environment God puts us in. We must be ready and willing to plant our wisdom and experience into others in the same way the butterfly stays on the lookout for new leaves to lay eggs on. We are our brother's keepers. We must live to triumph to help the next caterpillar become a beautiful, unique butterfly!

Yes, I am in Love with Jesus! While I was being molded and shaped, I never would have thought that greatness can come from a place of hurt. I was hurting from flooding memories of my abusive past, one which no one deserved to have done to them. I didn't deserve such abusive torment, physical or verbal abuse. These memories became something I thought I would have to carry for the rest of my life. But God! God began to order my steps by leading and guiding me in the direction he needed for me to be. As God replaced my fear with his faith, I began renewing my mind.

I started with forgiveness. I had to learn how to forgive people, including the same people who physically and verbally abused me. I had to learn that I could do "all things through Christ that strengthens me." Believe me, this wasn't easy at all, but the reward was great. From a girl who was called broke and poor to a woman with multiple successful businesses, taught by God to produce millions in those businesses. It was not until I was being transformed from a caterpillar into a butterfly that I finally found who I was. Broken by the hands of men, and now I walk in His image.

About
Lakina Fulks

Lakina Fulks is an Author of many books, a wife and mother of six children, she is a businesswoman; an entrepreneur who has many different businesses. She graduated with her Bachelor's in Business and Master's Degree in Social Justice. She believes in justice and doing what's right, and that all people should be treated fairly. She speaks for those who can't or are afraid to speak for themselves. She is a giving person and loves to help people. Lakina is a Vice President of The Lost and Found Christian Association. Their mission is to provide battered and sexually abused women and their children a rehabilitation process that includes continuity of care and empowerment. She is a part of the Women's Council of Realtors, along with a VIP Member of the International Associate of Professional Women.

Lakina is the founder of The Treasure Within, a 501(c)3 non-profit organization that was designed for young ladies age 8-19. The program is intended to motivate, empower, uplift, build self-esteem and teach leadership skills, and for the ladies to find the treasure within them so they can recognize their goals, dreams, and desires for their lives, www.thetreasurewithinyou.org. Lakina recently started a talk show called Believe in Yourself Tuesday that is featured on the SMD live Network, Iheart radio, and her YouTube channel

Lakina Fulks. She believes there are hidden treasures in everyone, and everyone is special and has gifts. She is big on Faith and the power of believing. She loves to empower all people to be the best they can be.

(248) 270-2916 | lakinatheauthor@gmail.com
www.lakinatheauthor.com

THE DREAM
THE
NIGHTMARE
AND
THE MIRACLE

PROPHETESS JOYCE HOGAN

THE SPIRIT of the Lord God is upon me because the Lord has anointed and qualified me to preach the Gospel of good tidings to the meek, the poor, and afflicted. He has sent me to bind up and heal the brokenhearted, to proclaim liberty to the [physical and spiritual] captives and the opening of the prison and of the eyes to those who are bound. (Isaiah 61:1 AMPC)

Apostle Hogan sensed the move of God stirring within him. The Lord revealed to him that he would be a senior leader - in other words - he would be a Pastor. Not wanting to be disobedient or miss the timing of God, he prayerfully considered what God was saying to him. The call of ministry was upon his life for some time, and now he was sensing it was time to move forward. The timing had to be right.

Wednesday evenings were our prayer and Bible Study nights. On this particular night no one showed up to Bible Study except for our Senior Pastor, Charles Hawthorne, and my husband. That night, Pastor Hawthorne felt that God was calling him back to Ann Arbor to build a church. He spoke these words to my husband that night. He said to him, "What God has for Detroit - maybe you have it." After revealing what was on his heart and the call of God to our senior leader that night, he was released by our Pastor to go ahead and do what the Lord called him to do. He blessed him with the release and in many other ways.

In 1994, we moved forward with God's leading to start Living Bread Ministries (LBM). That name was given to my husband 15 years prior, but the timing did not occur until 1994.

Within one year, we purchased our first building on Seven Mile Road in Detroit, Michigan. We were excited about how God was moving in the ministry because of obedience to his voice. It was evident God was a blessing and moving among us, but we felt there was something more for us spiritually He was wanting us to have. At that time, one of the members told Apostle about a meeting going on. Pastor Yoder was having Bill Hamon and John Eckhardt in to preach. He decided to go, and while he was there, they had a prophetic activation. This was so new to us. An activation is stirring up the Spirit of God within you for you to move in the prophetic.

It was new and exciting! Once there, he saw an old friend, John Eckhardt. After the service, they went out, and from there things began changing for us. In 1995, Apostle Eckhardt introduced us to the deliverance and prophetic ministries when he came to our church for a deliverance meeting. Also, different ministry leaders from his church, Crusaders Ministries, came and imparted to every area of our ministry.

One day, Apostle received a call from Apostle Eckhardt that he wanted to ordain him as an Apostle. This was not something my husband was trying to be or wanted to do, making it an unexpected honor. Apostle Eckhardt shared with him that he was led to ordain him. We traveled to Chicago along with several of our members for the ordination service. It was blessed. Soon after returning home, we began experiencing rapid growth until we eventually outgrew our 120-seat sanctuary.

We needed to find a larger space to accommodate all the many people who were coming. During that time, my parents closed their church to join our ministry. God was blessing. We began looking for a larger building to worship in. We drove around the city, but we kept being drawn to the area of Telegraph and Schoolcraft. We noticed a vacant building in a strip mall area. We did not get any information that day, but we kept being drawn back into that area by the Spirit of God. We inquired about it, and the owner worked with us to purchase it.

We had a dedication service when we completed the renovation of our new church home. It was a completely new facility with over 22,000 square feet, a classroom for our youth, and space to grow. In 2002, we moved in. At first, the larger space seemed awkward. Our praise dancers had to learn how to spread out, and the praise and worship team had to learn to adjust to the acoustics. We felt blessed, and we continued with rapid growth in our new location. There were the typical church problems but nothing that God could not handle.

Soon the ministry began growing again. We were able to make all our payments with no problem. Our hearts were so fixed on doing the work of the Lord. People were being set free, moving in the gifts of the Spirit, and growing spiritually. All was going well.

But within seven years we began seeing a change taking place in the ministry. Some members started to lose their jobs. There were lay-offs, and the church finances began to decrease despite continuing to have people join the church. We did not realize we were about to enter a trial that would test our faith to the very end. It would be a trial that separated those who believed and trusted God from those who chose to cower down to fear. It brought the pages of the Word of God right into your life. *"Trust in the Lord with all of your heart and lean not to your own understanding"* (Proverbs 3:5).

The Nightmare

In 2009, we entered a nightmare season for our church and our ministry financially. It started in 2008 when the Great Economic Recession began in our nation. It devastated the country, and in our city, it affected many individuals, companies, and churches. In particular, members of Living Bread Church were affected financially, drastically decreasing our monthly offerings and donations. This led to a

deficit in our monthly income. Many of the member's lives were changed financially, causing them to relocate to other states for employment. Eventually, we were forced into foreclosure on our church building. This brought a change numerically and financially for our ministry. Where the church was once able to pay all our bills on time - it was now a burden and financial struggle. When we purchased our building, we gutted and re-designed it to accommodate the needs of our congregation. Although we were blessed to have accomplished much for the Kingdom, our nightmare was only beginning. We had to learn to hold onto the Word of God and continue in faith to believe that He would bring us through.

We kept on praying and standing on the written Word as well as the spoken Word of God. We believed what He said to us and He was able to bring us through it all. Let me say that what you are standing and believing God to do for you and in your life is a walk of faith and trust in God. You must trust Him to the very end. This walk of faith is also warfare.

The battle is in the mind. You are fighting against every negative Word the enemy will bring to you. *"Fight the good fight of faith, lay hold on eternal life, whereunto thou art also called, and hast professed a good profession before many witnesses"* (1 Timothy 6:12 KJV). The word fight (*agōnizou*) means to agonize, struggle, battle, contend, and fight for the prize. It's the idea of a desperate effort and struggle. It was a struggle in the mind to fight against the voice of the enemy and the naysayers. We fought to keep our faith and to trust in the Word of God. Any saint who feels it is not a fight, I take my hat off to you. There will be times of intense wrestling with your thoughts and staying focused on what God said he would do.

We know that with God, nothing is impossible to him that believes. When you are going through, you must learn to stand on God's Word, to trust him and believe that He is a God that is able to do just what He said He would do. Do not ever get to the place where you say, what I believed was not for me because He did not come when I thought He should have. So many believers feel that their miracle or what they are believing for should be instant. It took us seven years. Many thought we had lost our minds. They were saying that it does not take all of that praying, all that warfare or fasting. Yes, we had to get ourselves to a place where we believed God.

On June 3, 2012, we received an official foreclosure notice on our building. It was posted on the door of the church. That Sunday morning, the person who opened the doors of the church placed the foreclosure notice under Apostle's office door. Getting a foreclosure notice was one of the things we were hoping would not happen. That Sunday, Apostle did not reveal anything regarding the foreclosure until after the service. You would have never known by the way he ministered that anything was wrong. The fight was beginning to intensify. We were struggling with payments here and there, trying to hold on to our building from 2009 until we received the official notice of foreclosure in 2012.

After service, on our way home, Apostle gave me the devastating news. It was something we knew was inevitable. The hurt and pain of hearing about the official foreclosure papers was overwhelming for me. We knew the warfare was increasing and that we had to continue in faith. You see, in 2011, I made a covenant with God that I would rise every morning at 5 a.m. and pray for my husband. I knew that he was under a heavy burden from the cares of the ministry. That hour in prayer was focused on my husband. I asked God to strengthen him, give him favor, and understanding in all that he had to do for the ministry and in business affairs.

A few days later, the realtor put up a For Sale sign on the building. Almost immediately we began receiving calls from people wanting to know what happened. One of Apostle's friends called my husband. During the conversation, he said to Apostle Hogan, "God is up to something." Those words were so prophetic at that moment. They resonated in my spirit. I began to have hope that God was up to something. However, we still had to go through the foreclosure process. The whole process was a walk of faith. Even though it was foreclosed, we were trying to rent the building. At times it was difficult to make the monthly payments. It was a few days before we revealed anything to the members about the foreclosure and how we had to be strong and continue believing and trusting God to bring us out.

On June 10, 2012, during a Sunday morning service, the Prophets in the house had a word for us that day. I thank God for the prophets. God revealed the secrets and what He was about to do with us, to us, and among us. *"Surely the Lord GOD will do nothing, but he revealed his secret unto his servants the prophets"* (Amos 3:7 KJV).

My heart was heavy that Sunday morning as I was walking into church with many thoughts going through my mind. Will we be able to worship in this place where God told us to go? As I walked in, I reminded myself what the Lord had spoken to me in my prayer time with Him.

I would remind myself that he had our backs and that we would not lose our church. I would tell myself not to worry. Yes, but the enemy was working, and just as quickly as I received the Word of the Lord, the enemy was right behind, bringing doubt and fear to me. I was concerned if we would have a place for the people of God to worship. Has all the work and financial resources given for the building now coming to an end? As I stood in the worship service, I focused my mind and heart on worship and praise unto the Lord.

You see, I desperately needed a word from God that day. I felt the weight of the ministry and my husband on my shoulders. I knew of the struggle to get where we were. But praise and worship allowed my mind to forget about what we faced ahead of us. I focused my heart and mind on the Lord and worshiped Him. Worshiping is a way for me to enter into the presence of the Lord and be at his throne. The praise and worship team were singing, and the praises of God filled the atmosphere. The Spirit of the Lord began to move on the Prophets. As the Prophets began giving the Word of the Lord, I was so ready to hear what God wanted to reveal unto us.

The first Word that came from one of the Prophets of the church was for the entire congregation.

"I hear the Father say, my sons and my daughters. I hear the Lord say, don't you know that this is the hour of praise and worship. This is the hour that I am causing your enemies to be defeated. I hear the Lord say, why are you standing so far away from me? God says I'm here. I'm here to take you through. I'm here. This is your day of victory. I hear the Lord

say, where is my praise? Where is my Worship? God said, did not I say that it is a weapon? The Lord says, Shake it off! Shake it off! Says the Lord ... And then I heard the Lord say, the enemy wants to take your focus. He wants to cause you to look to the right and look to the left, but did not I say to you to look at me. So, look up my sons and my daughters and begin to praise me. Praise me, for I am your God! Praise me, for I am your God! Praise me, for I am your God! I am your God!"

~Prophetic Word spoken by one of the Prophets

This is a portion of the second Word that stood out to Apostle and me. This Word was given directly to us.

"The Father told me to tell you mighty man of God, the general on the inside of you, the apostolic and the prophetic anointing, the Lord said to speak to the Apostle in you and tell you, man of God, because you stepped back and let him render what he wanted to render, you opened up the governmental authority of God. You began to open and break the ranks of hell against Living Bread. Your obedience brought obedience into the house, saith the Lord. And the Lord says, Apostle, this day he wants you to ask a favor of him, you and Prophetess Joyce. The Lord says, son, I want to wake up again the apostolic in you. I want to charge you son. It's not over. You will not lose this church. You will not lose nothing that I give you. Just ask of me this day. This day son, the Lord says, stir up every tongue and give him his word back Apostle."

~Prophetic Word spoken by one of the Prophets

The words that were released that day came from the throne room of God. Those words blessed us; reassuring us that God sees, He hears, and He will deliver. That was just a few of the prophetic words that were given to us over several years that we stood on - believing and trusting Him. There were so many reassurances of what He was going to do and did do for us.

We continued renting the building, still trusting that God would bring us out of it all. It was not overnight that we received our deliverance or miracle. But God was faithful to help us through each process. *"For the eyes of the LORD run to and fro throughout the whole earth, to show Himself strong on behalf of those whose heart is loyal to Him"*

(2 Chronicles 16:9a NKJV). The congregation joined their faith with our faith, believing that God was able to bring us through it all. We were trusting Him with all we had and were not leaning on our own understanding. We couldn't even begin to comprehend what God had planned in store for us, or even the warfare that was ahead of us. But we would not give up. We believed Him for the miracle.

THIRTY DAY NOTICE

We were still in our building in 2015. Apostle was trying to obtain a mortgage so we could buy back our building, to no avail. No lending institution would give us a mortgage to re-purchase the building. The banks were already holding onto loans they had foreclosed on. Businesses, churches, and homes had been foreclosed on during that time. The company that owned the mortgage on our building was trying to work with us, but once the sign was placed on our building, realtors started showing the property. It was heartbreaking to see that sign on the property. Now with the sign on the property, it brought in Pastors who wanted to view it. The devastation of seeing another congregation going through the property was overwhelming for me.

The Apostle made sure they didn't show it on the days we had our intercessory prayer. I wanted the intercessors to keep the faith. Each time the Realtors would show the property, the Pastors going through would ask to speak with Apostle. They would ask him, "Why are you selling the church?" He would explain to them that we are not selling it and how the bank foreclosed on us. He explained how the mortgage company was no longer going to wait for us to obtain a mortgage to purchase back our building.

God gave him favor with each Pastor that he was able to speak with, and they would not be interested. Or some would say, "I will not touch this building. It belongs to this congregation."

There were a few months with no communication between Apostle and the person handling our account during the time of the foreclosure. Apostle was sensing in his Spirit that something was going on with the realtor and the mortgage company.

On September 14, 2015, we received a termination of the lease agreement with the company that held our mortgage. We were told to vacate no later than midnight on October 14, 2015, at which time we were to surrender all the keys and security codes to the property. Our building had been sold to another congregation that had not personally gone through our building. They had only looked at the pictures. Apostle made a phone call to the one working with us. He confirmed the letter that was sent, and he said they had a buyer and a substantial deposit on the building.

The spiritual warfare was beginning to increase again. The Apostle said to the person handling our mortgage, "I think I will get an attorney." The lender stated to Apostle, "I was hoping we did not have to go that way."

After he finished talking with him, Apostle came up the stairs to give me the news. I could tell by his steps that it was not good. As he entered the room, he told me the devastating news that our church had been sold. I was in disbelief, in shock, and upset. Hundreds of emotions were going through my mind. My knees hit the floor. They could not support me. My body went numb. I felt as if the floor had been removed from underneath me. Apostle tried to catch me as I was going down and helped me into my chair in the bedroom. Tears began to flow down my face. I cried out, "Father, what happened?" Apostle informed me that he had to leave to go and take care of a few things. I did not know that he had already contacted an attorney before we even heard the news of selling the church. I told him to go and that I would be okay.

I was glad he left because I needed to talk to God. I needed some answers. I was home alone. I was still sitting in my green chair when I began presenting my case before the Lord. I said, "Father, what happened? You said you had our back. We would not lose the church. We would not lose anything that you have given us. We stood on your Word, preached your Word, and believed the Word." Well, He knows our thoughts anyway. Why not express your feelings? In Hebrews, it says, *for we do not have a High Priest who cannot sympathize with our weaknesses, but was in all points tempted as we are, yet without sin.* (Hebrews 4:15 NKJV).

Jesus is touched by our feelings. He knows and understands that there is just so much we can handle because we're flesh. We were designed to depend totally upon him, our creator. *"Trust in the LORD with all your heart, and lean not on your own understanding; in all your ways acknowledge Him, And He shall direct your paths"* (Proverb 3:4-5 NKJV).

Trusting God is being totally dependent on him. It's knowing that he will somehow bring you through the trial you are going through. We must trust Him completely. We heard the voice of God in our prayer time. Prophetic words were given to us, and we had His written Word. We said God cannot lie. God has given both his promise and his oath. *"These two things are unchangeable because it is impossible for God to lie. Therefore, we who have fled to him for refuge can have great confidence as we hold to the hope that lies before us"* (Hebrews 6:18 (NLT).

After receiving the 30-day notice, we did not pack one box or move one piece of furniture. We were determined to see a miracle and see God move for us.

The Turnaround

We fought many spiritual battles during that time. My husband was in court for the next six months. It was a spiritual and emotional battle for us. We still had to stand and believe God through each court battle. The Word says to endure hardness as a good solider. *"Thou, therefore, endure hardness, as a good soldier of Jesus Christ"* (2 Timothy 2:3 KJV).

Every court case tested our faith in God, but we were determined to trust him to the very end. There was no turning back now.

We won the first battle in District Court. We were glad and felt like everything was going in our favor. Our attorney informed us that it's like playing chess. You make a move, and they will make a move. Sure enough, after a few weeks we were back in court, this time in Circuit Court. We had an agreement with the lender, which the Judge ruled null and void.

After several court appearances, the lenders were given the right to move forward with the sale of the property to the buyers. The last court appearance in which the Judge ruled against LBM was devastating to Apostle. He sat with his head down in disbelief as he listened to the judge rule against us. He was exhausted, at the end of his rope, and felt totally let down by God. He felt that God had left him out there to be destroyed. Every time he was in prayer, the Lord said that we would win. He had believed, stood on the Word, and trusted the Lord. But in his heart, he kept asking the Lord, "Why? Are we going to lose this battle?" His heart was heavy that day as he sat listening to the Judge. He could hear the whispers from the lender's representative, saying, "Yes!"

On his way home, he called me and gave me the news. When Apostle came home, he was despondent. He came in, spoke to me, and went straight upstairs to change his clothes and go into his prayer room.

He got on his face before the Lord and began wrestling with God in prayer. He wept, refusing to be denied the manifestation of all the words that God had spoken. We were not going to give up or let this die. I knew deep inside that God's Word was true. The devil thought he had won. I even heard the enemy challenging my God, "Your God said he was going to give you back your church." I could see the faces of all our members and heard them saying, "Apostle, you told us that God said... And what about all of the prophetic words that came forth?"

While I stood believing God for a miracle, I wrestled with those words that He spoke to me many days. I felt like Jacob wrestling in prayer with God. In prayer, there is always a place of solitude with God - telling him your needs and telling Him that we need His help. He would go before the Lord and remind him of his written Word and the prophetic words that he had given to us. "You will not lose this church or anything that I have given you." Our faith was in God; that He was working things out. When it looks the darkest, you still have to stand and trust that God is working things out in your favor.

"Faith means that we are certain of the things we hope for, convinced of the things we do not see." (William Barclay commentary)

"Some trust in chariots, and some in horses: but we will remember the name of the LORD our God." (Psalm 20:7 KJV)

Your victory is in God and his power. He will defeat your enemy. You have to trust him, depend on him. Never give up but stand on his Word. We stood and believed God, not on what we were facing, but based on God's Word regardless of

what our sight showed us. Deep down in our hearts we said God's Word is true. We began to rehearse many of our trials and how God delivered us. We spoke to each other that we will not give up; we will fight this battle on our knees, trust God.

The Phone Call

A few days later, on a Wednesday, we were at 12-noon prayer. Apostle was in his office when he received a phone call from a Bishop friend of his who had gone through a similar situation with his church and won his battle. He stated to Apostle that the Lord spoke to him while he was on vacation. He told him to call Apostle and give him this Word. *"The Lord said, you will not lose your church for God said, 'I will vindicate you.'"* We had already received the verdict from the Judge in favor of the lender. But this is just like God. *"Things that are impossible with man are possible with God"* (Luke 18:27 (KJV).

After their conversation, thirty minutes later Bishop called Apostle again. This time he said to Apostle, "I know who is buying your church." Bishop stated, "I called him and said to him, 'God said that is not your church. That church belongs to Apostle Kenneth Hogan.'" Bishop went on to say, "I gave the purchasing Pastor your number, and he is going to call you."

This was God working behind the scenes. Things we think are impossible to man are possible with God. Apostle had favor with this purchaser and everyone who came through to see the building. They would ask to talk with him, and after he explained what was happening, they would say they were stepping back. But we had no way of knowing who was purchasing it or when they had a chance to go through the building. But God knew who and how it happened. The next day Apostle received a call from the purchasing Pastor...

About Dr. Joyce M. Hogan

Dr. Joyce M. Hogan serves alongside her husband as Pastors of Living Bread Ministries, Int'l. She holds a doctorate in Theology and decades of ministry experience and wisdom. She is the author of *Characteristics of an Intercessor*, and *60 Days in His Presence*.

Dr. Hogan serves as the leader of the prayer ministry at their church. Gifted with a strong prophetic call, she both hosts and ministers at various women's conferences. She has a heart for women and a desire to raise up godly women who are strong in the Lord, loving to their husbands and committed to their families. Dr. Hogan resides in the Detroit area with her husband and has two married adult children, along with three grandchildren.

There can be no victory without a battle. Courage is hidden when things are going well. When all the glory, honor, and praise, points to Jesus Christ, our Lord, then his light shines in the darkness to draw others to him that they will be blessed.

joyce0620@aol.com

WWW.LBMWESTGATE.ORG

VIEW FROM THE PEW:HOW TO SURVIVE A CHURCH HURT

BARBRA GENTRY-PUGH

As a Believer in Christ, I have had the privilege of experiencing some amazing and transformative moments within the local church. I was blessed to be reared in a Christian home where the biblical principles of God's Word were taught and demonstrated. My father was a preacher of the gospel of Jesus Christ from as far back as I can remember. He was my Pastor for most of my young adult life, and attending church, Bible study, and participating in ministry was the norm. As a result, I am acutely familiar with "*church work*" along with the "*work of the church*." Growing up in church was a rewarding part of my life, and I was blessed to experience and participate in many church activities, ministries, and programs that grounded and helped shape me into the woman I am today. For that, I am profoundly grateful!

Even as there are numerous rewarding moments as a Believer in Christ, there are also painful moments that exist and occur within the local church that can change the trajectory of one's life forever. Most often, these moments and occurrences are unexpected, so there is no preparing or bracing yourself for them.

It became noticeably clear to me that the more involved and committed I became to the life and culture of church ministry, the more *vulnerable* I was to various *attacks* which often precipitated moments of unquestionable and undeniable hurt. Make no mistake, being in ministry or participating in church does not exempt you from being wounded. Sometimes these ill moments will be experienced and viewed from the church pew, positioning you to suffer in silence for the sake of the ministry.

This silence is often deadly because of what happens deep in the fabric of one's mind, heart, and soul when you are wounded this way. Church hurt has many different faces! Have you ever been hurt verbally by a pastor, church leader, or another Believer who fellowshipped with you in church? Have you been betrayed, humiliated, misrepresented, or embarrassed from the pulpit by a pastor or other church representative? Have you felt beat-up from the pulpit and wondered why the leader, speaker, or minister did not have the courage to speak directly to you, send you an email, text, or even call you before calling you out? If they really felt you needed help, guidance, or correction, why would they not reach out directly?

If they genuinely cared about your soul, and your Christian growth and maturity, why would they crush your spirit in that manner? Has a committee member ever lied to the pastor about you because of their jealousy towards you? Have you ever just sat in church, needing to hear a Word from the Lord and was let down because all you got was ranting and raving from the pulpit and rock-throwing where you were completely oblivious to the context and had no interest in the matter?

What perplexed me in the many years of my church life is seeing men and women called, anointed, and appointed, who refuse to be used by God to His greatest potential in them. We all have issues, and when we do not allow God to help us deal with, address, and resolve them, He cannot use us fully and be glorified in us the way He truly deserves.

Wounded by The People of God

One of the most devasting and painful experiences in my life was the result of "*Church Hurt*." As a ministry leader in a local church, the venomous words spoken from the pulpit during that historic Sunday morning worship service pierced my heart. I had been singled out once again, but why? I could not understand why my efforts to serve the Lord and be a vessel for HIS glory was such an irritant to those around me.

There always seemed to be a bit of criticism, no matter what direction I took. Though I offered the gift God had given me with joy, I always felt betrayed, devalued, and maligned. I was even accused of teaching heresy. The only reason I could conceive for such a charge was because of my choice to avail myself of external Biblical teachings from Bible Study Fellowship International, Birmingham Bible Institute, Tyndale Bible College, and my graduating from the Michigan Theological Seminary. Somehow, they thought all these things posed a threat to the pulpit. However, I love God and His Word. I desired to represent and be used by Him, and continually seeking and receiving knowledge is a part of that. Although my name was never mentioned in the sermon, there was only one "*President of the Women's Ministry*," and it was me. Thus, if those words would have been sent certified mail, I would have been the one to personally sign for them.

Normally, one would have a reasonable expectation that the preached Word will encourage, support, and instruct you on how to live out the Christian life, but I didn't feel any of those things that Sunday morning. Do not get me wrong, I know the institution of the church is made up of imperfect people, and that the church, the Body of Christ, is not perfect either. No one is expected to be made perfect from attending the Sunday worship service.

I just want you to know and be reminded that there are dysfunctional and imperfect people attending every time the church doors are open. They range from seasoned saints to new babes in Christ. Some are looking for church membership while others are just spectators. Some are Christians deficient in their faith, and some have been battered and bruised by life and need comfort from the Lord, His Word, and His people.

So, what is "*Church Hurt*?" Being in the church all my life, a clear and all-encompassing definition has been a challenge to come up with, so let's tackle it based on my experiences. *Church Hurt* is when a leader or leaders, or others in the local church do and/or say something to deliberately hurt you or damage your character. These individuals refuse to receive you or what you stand for. Instead, they make a conscious decision not to engage in any dialogue with you to gain clarity or learn the rationale behind your position before lording their position upon you. In some cases, even if there is dialogue, it is a mere formality, and their hearts and minds are already set against you.

They cannot even agree to disagree in love and mutual respect. Never underestimate how pettiness and small-mindedness can destroy relationships, in or outside of the church. So, how does *Church Hurt show itself? Some of the ways it comes across are through a lack of compassion,* insensitivity, critical and accusatory language, and ungodly badgering that chips away at the fiber of your soul. It is the result of dogmatism, selfishness fueled by insecurity, inflexibility, blame, and an inferiority complex. Believe me when I say, it's not okay to pardon this ill behavior towards yourself and others with *"Well, that's just how they are. I'll just overlook it."*

Is it ever okay to turn a blind eye on abuse or the mistreatment of others? Being the leader of a Women's Ministry with a love of God and a passion to Know HIM, the heartbeat of His Voice, and His Word, I envisioned ministry as being much more than social activities. I longed to see women living out their faith more effectively, as life is real! I knew and talked to women who came to church hurting and went home hurting!

As I listened to their struggles and issues, I felt compelled to do more. I sought to provide opportunities for women to come and know God's love as they learned more about living unpretentious and godly lives. I attempted to create an atmosphere for women of all ages who were facing real-life challenges where they could be provided with real-life solutions and opportunities to live holistic and balanced lives through transformational relationships with the heart of God so they could be better women, wives, mothers, and citizens of the kingdom. The heartbeat of women's ministry is empowering women to share, grow and mature in all areas of their lives, physically, emotionally, socially, financially, and spiritually; and to follow God intimately, serve Him authentically, and share Him confidently with others who do not know Him as their Lord and Savior, Jesus Christ. My passion to see women become fulfilled in their purpose caused my heart to struggle in my relationship with some in the church. It appeared that some women were not sure or knowledgeable about their purpose and viewed the things of God as unimportant. Even more difficult to grasp was the reality that other women did not seem to recognize that living out their faith involved doing more than just going to scheduled church services. It was a long time before I accepted that not all believers in Christ understood their purpose or valued their faith!

Christ gave His life for us, and He has a plan for each of our lives. This season of my life caused me to walk more closely with the Lord than ever before. Consequently, my faith became stronger, and I grew more solid in the courage of my convictions. I was also better able to allow others to be who they choose to be, trusting God to love them through their difficulties as He has done with me.

Burying my husband and one of my best friends unexpectedly within six months of each other was such a blow! I was still going through the grieving process and needed to be nurtured and refreshed by love and the Word of God. In an attempt to soothe my aching heart, I attended Sunday worship service since it had always been a necessary source of my strength and support. However, this occasion would yield something different.

After hearing the words splattered from the pulpit in the previous service, I was unwilling to endure any more unnecessary pain. I was badgered from the pulpit, and it wounded me terribly. It felt as if my heart was bleeding, and I could hardly breathe. It was then that I knew at some point I would have to leave that church and that ministry. Life is hard; we all get hurt from time to time, but this was more than I could bear.

As a Certified Biblical Counselor and Registered Nurse for over forty years, I was keenly aware that bleeding of any nature, if not attended to, whether physical, emotional, or spiritual, will eventually lead to life-threatening consequences. As I sat in the church pew, it was as if something was moving my body. I stood up and could hear a still clear voice saying to me, "It is time to leave." There was no doubt in my mind this was the voice of God, and it was perfect timing! It was now the time of the congregational fellowship, so I gave my tithes and building fund offering envelopes to my friend and asked her to turn them in. Then I walked out of the church.

Words are not sufficient to express what and how I felt as I drove home from church that afternoon. Although my heart ached, I was breathing better, despite knowing I was leaving behind over seven years of women's ministry work, the design of the Women's Ministry's Logo God had given me, years of work spent designing a Ministry Manual for committee members, PowerPoint presentations, program flyers, Women's Conference format and contacts, along with all the women I would dearly miss and do miss to this day. Fortunately, I continue fellowshipping with some of them today! By the time I arrived home, there was such a sense of relief.

I felt at least 20 pounds lighter. I was free. I could breathe better, and my heart was no longer hurting. I just felt numb.

As a student of the Word of God, I understand clearly what the Bible says about "The Church," the Bride of Christ, and its purpose. Throughout the New Testament, God declared why He established HIS church! Let's take a look:

Acts 2:42 NLT says, "All the believers devoted themselves to the apostles' teaching, and to fellowship, and to sharing in meals (including the Lord's Supper), and to prayer."
1. teaching biblical doctrine
2. providing a place of fellowship for believers
3. observing the Lord's supper, and
4. praying.
Ephesians 4:14.
- The church is to teach biblical doctrine, so we can be grounded in our faith (Romans 12:9-10).
- The church is to be a place of fellowship, where Christians can be devoted to one another and honor one another (Romans 15:14).
- The church is to be a place to receive instruction and support for one another (Ephesians 4:32.)
- The church is to be kind and compassionate to one another (1 Thessalonians 5:11).
- The church *is to encourage one another* (1 John 3:11).
- The church *is to love one another* (1 Corinthians 11:23b-26]

- The church is to be a place where believers can observe the Lord's Supper, remembering Christ's death and the shedding of his blood on our behalf (Matthew 28:18-20).
- The church is called to be faithful in sharing the gospel to the world (James 1:27).
- The church is to be about the business of ministering to those in need.

- I don't see any place where God said to take time out from the message of the gospel to conduct *"church discipline, venting, or anything else."* He sent Jesus to this earth to do one thing, and that is to seek and save the lost.

"For the Son of Man came to seek and save those who are lost." (Luke 19:10 NLT)

Let me be clear, people are not hurt in every church; however, most churches have hurt someone at some point. Remember, we are sinners, saved by His grace, and a work in progress. The local church is a place to come and be healed through the preached Word, fellowship, and prayer.

Wounds ~ Woundedness

During my nursing career, I have taken care of all types of physical wounds in all stages of healing. Some were potentially, serious wounds with foul purulent drainage. No matter what type or stage of the wound, if it is going to heal it _must_ have meticulous and consistent care. By now, you may be asking, what does *wound care* have to do with *church hurt*? It has everything to do with it. *Church hurt* has produced serious *emotional and spiritual wounds*. These wounds can be deep and penetrating, and if not properly treated with the Word of God and His infinite wisdom, they can become infected. The handling of these wounds is especially crucial, and any improper response can cause even more hurt. Just like the care of *physical wounds*, care and treatment of *emotional and spiritual wounds* requires the same meticulous and consistent care. Left untreated, these wounds can fester into infections of anger, bitterness, resentment, grief, brokenness, and often shame. The result of infectious wounds has been seen in families and various groups where the infected, painful wound went on to cause division and fighting, even from past generations. This affects the church, the Body of Christ.

"Then they cried to the LORD in their trouble, and he delivered them from their distress. He sent out his word and healed them and delivered them from their destruction."
(Psalm 107:19-20 ESV)

One thing you can count on, you will experience pain in this life. It may be temporarily discomforting or permanently disabling, even life-threatening or deadly. I was acutely aware that I was suffering from deep emotional and spiritual wounds. No matter what type of wound you may experience, physical, emotional, or spiritual, there is trauma. My emotional wounds were painful, and I experienced a tearing and crushing of my feelings, passions, and expressions. My *spiritual wounds* were also deep. Although I periodically attended church, the Word of God never appeared to penetrate because the deep wounds of my heart refused to heal.

Wounds inflicted by the people of God are especially painful as you do not expect to be hurt by God's people. Be mindful that wounds from God's people are not the same as wounds caused by the enemy of God. Treating wounds of this type often involves a different process as it relates to healing and wholeness. Many have heard the phrase, *"Hurting people, hurt others."* I would like to also say that *"Wounded people, Wound other people."* Their actions are often driven by pride, ambition, lust, jealousy, greed, selfishness, insecurity, guilt, and unforgiveness. Our Savior was wounded. In fact, my Lord and Savior knows just how I feel because He experienced the pain of the cross, suffered, and died for me. *"But he was wounded for our transgressions, he was bruised for our iniquities; the chastisement of our peace was upon him; and with his stripes we are healed."* (Isaiah 53:5 ASV)

The Turning Point

Shortly after walking out of the church, I decided to give them my resignation. Driving away from the church, I felt like I was getting closure to that chapter of my life; however, I very quickly realized this was only the beginning of my journey towards healing. I have been told, "Barbra, you can be rather naïve," and of course I would disagree. I just do not understand why people who claim to love God can't seem to love God's people. You are probably saying, "Yes, *the sister is naïve!*" I shared with my brother, Rev. Michael E. Gentry, that I had resigned from the church. He was not surprised and proceeded to inform me that I needed to do the right thing and meet with my former Pastor. I thought to myself, *Lord, why do I need to do that?* I knew he was right, but I simply wasn't ready to do that.

The Holy Spirit convicted me, and I made an appointment to meet with him. I asked my friend to go with me. I did not need a mediator, just a witness. After meeting with him, it provided me with confirmation that I had obeyed God. Some of our discussion felt as if salt was being poured into my already open wound, and my passion for women and the women's ministry was being misconstrued.

After leaving the pastor's office, I was able to admit to myself that I was still angry, hurt, and felt mistreated; however, the meeting helped me to experience and accept my deep emotional and spiritual wounds. Continuing to dress my wounds meant I would continue suffering and living in denial of my sins. I would never be able to fully walk in my purpose, being damaged and wounded. I did not want to be another wounded Believer in ministry, going about wounding other Believers. I did not want to be like a physical wound with purulent drainage oozing and getting all over others.

I continued visiting other churches periodically to hear the preached Word. I must be honest, there were some worship services where I could not wait to get out and go home. I knew in my heart I was not healed, and I certainly wasn't ready for church membership. *Healing is a process.* Just as the healing of a deep physical wound will not happen overnight, the same holds true for emotional and spiritual wounds. I don't care how nice the dressing looks on the outside; when wounds are not properly treated the tissue underneath will die, causing the healthy tissue to also die. Untreated emotional and spiritual wounds will respond in the same way. I knew I was not prepared to help or minister to anyone. Just like clean dressing over a deep wound,

I was nicely dressed with some deep emotional and spiritual wounds, unhealed, draining, and foul. I was bleeding all over my friends about what happened and needed to be healed and delivered. I did not want to continue walking around with open wounds bearing a foul odor. My heart's desire was always to please God and be a good representative of the Lord Jesus Christ.

"From the sole of the foot even to the head, there is no soundness in it, but bruises and sores and raw wounds; they are not pressed out or bound up or softened with oil." (Isaiah 1:6 ESV)

I Am Free ~ No Longer Bound
Freedom cannot be purchased! I don't care how rich you are, the only way emotional and spiritual wounds can be healed is by employing the Master Healer. The unadulterated Word of God and the power of the Holy Spirit healed me.

"He sent out his word and healed them, snatching them from the door of death. Let them praise the LORD for his great love and for the wonderful things he has done for them." (Psalm 107:20-21 NLT)

It took exactly one year to be a vessel that God could use again for His glory. God did the healing His way by eventually giving me something to do. He sat me down to write my first book, *Every Beat of My Heart*. God used this to perform open-heart surgery on me. Some of the specific chapters God used to heal me were, *The Heartbeat of Adversity, The Heartbeat of Emotional Pain, The Heartbeat of Forgiveness, The Heartbeat of Transformation*, and others.

With each chapter, He opened my wounds, cleansing them of the old necrotic tissue and then applying His ointment of the Word of God. The graciousness of God walked me back through my hurts. Through His infinite wisdom, He aided me in differentiating between what Jesus Christ accomplished at Calvary and the ongoing work of sanctification by the Holy Spirit in me! He reminded me of who He is in my life and who I am in Him.

He is my heavenly Father, and I am His child. He will NEVER reject me, and He loves me with an undying love. During this time of sitting before the Lord, reading, and being sifted by His Word, meditating on His Word, and writing, God taught me that He could meet me in the sanctuary of my home. The Holy Spirit taught me what He wanted me to know, and that I can offer HIM a sacrifice of praise from the fruit of my lips no matter where I am. Be reminded, the only place of safety is in the arms of Jesus.

Whatever process God uses to heal you, immediately embrace it. Wounds MUST be healed early to be a ready vessel to minister without guilt and shame. Make a decision; you can hurt or be healed. It is a choice!
Start by admitting you are hurting and in need of healing. Do not walk around for days, months, or even years with untreated wounds and allow them to become a stronghold in your life. I am a witness. God uses those He has healed to minister to those who are hurting.

1. EMPLOY God, the Master Physician, the Master Healer. You cannot do anything by yourself.
2. FORGIVE yourself and others. Forgiveness is rooted in love!
3. PRAY for divine direction for your life, and do not take one step unless it is ordered by God! This is your personal journey with a personal God.
4. SURRENDER to His prescription (Rx, the Bible) and do exactly what HE tells you to do.
5. REPENT for known sin.
6. RECEIVE God's Love and Restoration

God measures our pain to make us whole!

About a year later, I was attending a women's conference at a local church when I met a dear sister who befriended me and invited me to go to Bible Study with her. I shared with her that I did not want to leave the conference; however, I promised to visit her church on Sunday. The following Sunday, I attended her church and felt refreshed by the preached Word of God. I decided that I would like to attend the Bible Study. After several months of consistently attending worship services and Bible Study, I made the decision to get up from my seat to become a member, I was finally FREE!

"So, if the Son sets you free, you are truly free.
(John 8:36 NLT)

God singles us out to serve but training is required to get us to wholeness where the gift is transferred from one to another. The wholeness comes when everything is counted, weighed, measured, and considered, with nothing omitted. Preparing us for HIS service may include a journey through "Church Hurt!"

About Barbra R. Gentry-Pugh

Barbra R. Gentry-Pugh Founder and CEO of Heart Expressions Ministries International, LLC. Barbra is an international published award-winning author - a *recipient of the PWN International Literary Award* for her first book *"Every Beat of My Heart",* her debut book release. *She is an also contributing author* to seven books with The Professional Woman Network (PWN), a Certified Biblical Counselor, **Certified International Life Coach** *and a graduate of* Michigan Theological Seminary, with a Master's Degree in Christian Education.

(248) 302-9128 | barbragp@gmail.com
www.beatofmyheart.org

THE DIAMOND IN MY DISSAPOINTMET

BETH WEBER

Disappointments! Like diamonds, they come in all shapes and sizes. No one likes them! We all avoid them, yet everyone knows the taste of this bitter pill. Webster defines DISAPPOINTMENT as a failure to meet our expectations or hope. With all the negative press on the downside of life, how could there possibly be a diamond in our disappointment?

My Own Worst Nightmare

I wondered this very thing in 1994 when an unexpected whirlwind tore through our family and shattered my life as I knew it. I plunged into a sea of agonizing grief when my son left home in protest over our house rules against underage drinking. A litany of unanswered questions ricocheted through my mind, churning up forgotten memories. My throat tightened as I recalled sharing my fears about losing a child with trusted friends.

GOD WOULD NEVER LET THAT HAPPEN TO ME BECAUSE HE KNOWS I COULD NEVER HANDLE IT. Words spoken in jest long before I knew Jesus slammed against my heart like a boomerang. My legs felt like putty. The world was in slow motion. As Job said, "WHAT I FEARED HAS COME UPON ME; WHAT I DREADED HAS HAPPENED TO ME" (Job 3: 25-26). Then it struck me. I AM LIVING MY OWN WORST NIGHTMARE!

The hardest part of living your own worst nightmare is that you never wake up. Perhaps, like me, you know what it feels like to live life on an emotional roller coaster, constantly vacillating between terror, anger, exasperation, grief, despair, and utter exhaustion. Beneath the torrents of raw emotion ran an agonizing undercurrent of heartbreak over my broken son and our fractured family.

For the next four years, our fledgling parenting skills were stretched to the limit. The more we cried about our son and prayed for him, the worse things got. He never felt the barbs of his destructive choices because he found refuge in the arms of the community, who viewed our tough love as no love. Those same people lost their passion for my son's cause when they asked him to leave because their son was going away to college.

This impending eviction brought a glimmer of hope when he came back home, but once again, the cyclone of alcohol addiction tore through our family. My husband and I found ourselves in the unthinkable position of having to protect our younger children from their brother. In desperation, we toyed with the idea of selling our home to pay for his long-term treatment. Unfortunately, we never got the chance. He refused our help, announcing he would rather live at The Salvation Army homeless shelter than submit to our rules. Like the heartbroken parents of the prodigal son, we acquiesced and honored his request.

Disappointment pierced my heart when he disappeared through our front door and walked toward the shelter, never looking back. Within four short years, my firstborn son spiralled downward from being a respected scholar-athlete with several college scholarships to a homeless man living under bridges and hopping boxcars across the country.

Last Call

A late-night phone call broke a painful two-year silence. My husband fumbled in the dark to answer the phone. The sadness in his eyes and apprehension in his raspy voice warned me to brace myself for another disappointment. My son's voice washed away years of fear, but within minutes I recognized the delusional noise of mental illness. I was torn as his words soothed my aching heart while ripping it apart at the same time. I endured his incoherent ramblings for the next hour, hoping for a glimmer of lucidity that never came. I told my son I loved him and handed the phone to my husband. When I laid my head on the pillow, I felt the warmth of my tears trickling down my face. I whispered to myself, I WILL ALWAYS LOVE YOU, MY SON. What I did not know that December 9, 2000, was this would be the last time I would hear my son's voice for many years.

On March 21, 2012, the ringing of my telephone broke a distressing twelve-year silence. "Do you have a son by the name of James?" the caller asked.

"Yes," I replied, "Why do you ask?"

She announced, "Your son has been burned in a fire. He is in a coma and on a respirator."

Smoldering embers of cautious optimism burst into flames of hope as she filled me in on all the details. Cupping the phone, I shouted to my husband in the kitchen in loud whispers. HE'S ALIVE, JIM. OUR JIMMY IS ALIVE! Twenty-three hours later and after crossing several state lines by way of planes, trains, and automobiles, we stood in the doorway of our son's room in the burn unit. It was surreal. I felt the unmistakable presence of God as I fought back tears and inched my way to the foot of his bed. My long-lost son lay trapped beneath a web of medical tubes and bulky dressings. I studied his face, counted his toes, and spent hours staring at his motionless body as he lay in a coma. I watched his chest rise and fall to the rhythmic surges of a respirator, contemplating his fate. My mind raced with unanswered questions about the missing pieces of his puzzling life of homelessness. As I kissed his cheeks and forehead again and again, I could not stop telling him I loved him. I held a vigil at my son's bedside, praying for a miracle. The intense pressure of reality felt like a lead shawl draped over my shoulders; with the fear of banishment looming like a cyclone on the distant horizon.

To my great joy, the storm never came. Upon awakening from his coma and recovering from the shock of seeing us, our son welcomed us back into his life. This proved to be both precious and painful. While I was delighted to witness the miraculous healing of his burns, I also saw the undeniable symptoms of the mental illness I had long suspected. Professionals call it a diagnosis, but I call it heartache because it robbed me of my firstborn and hijacked my treasured son. Do you love someone who suffers from mental illness?

Home Sweet Home

My time out west with my son provided me with the missing pieces I needed to create a sketchy timeline of his intriguing homeless life. Disappointment struck with a vengeance when I learned that a woody marsh was not merely the scene of the fire that threatened to take his life, it was the place my son called home. The vexing years of uncertainty now seemed curiously palatable compared to these newly discovered realities. My tireless efforts and well-laid plans for ongoing support after his discharge unravelled at the eleventh hour. God's plan included another gut-wrenching good-bye. He returned to the woods where he lived as a recluse, sleeping outside even when the temperatures plummet to 40 below zero. I savored the occasional luxury of hearing my son's voice when I called the local mission, but after several months he went missing again.

How Long?

When my son first left home, each day felt like I was dragging ironclad feet through thick mud. I wanted to crawl into bed and pull the covers over my head until it was over, but life marched on. I mustered enough strength to work eight hours, then dragged myself home and put dinner on the table. In the clutches of unyielding despair, love for my husband and children was the only thing that kept me from ending my life. David's prayer became mine when the scorching whirlwind raged on. He wrote, *"HOW LONG, O LORD? WILL YOU FORGET*

ME FOREVER? HOW LONG WILL YOU HIDE YOUR FACE FROM ME? HOW LONG MUST I WRESTLE WITH MY THOUGHTS AND EVERY DAY HAVE SORROW IN MY HEART? HOW LONG WILL MY ENEMY TRIUMPH OVER ME?" (Psalm 13:1-2).

I was convinced that if I could only know how long the storm would last, I could muster enough strength to survive. Months of discouragement, sorrow, anxiety, and defeat chipped away at my noble resolve. God answered my prayer through the inspiring words of the author of Hebrews, who wrote that Moses,

"...PERSEVERED BECAUSE HE SAW HIM WHO IS INVISIBLE" (Hebrews 11:27). God knew that knowing how long my troubles would last is meaningless information.

Instead of telling me how long it would last, He showed me HOW to outlast my troubles, no matter how long they last. He wanted me to see the Invisible God.

The Diamond in My Disappointment

When disappointment struck, I LOOKED at my circumstances and saw no way out. God began teaching me how to LOOK AT my disappointments but SEE Jesus. This changed the way I saw my disappointment. It reminds me of when my husband surprised me with a diamond ring on our 14th wedding anniversary. I looked at the diamond on my finger but saw the character and depth of my husband's love. The inner beauty of his faithfulness and kindness sparkled like the hidden facets deep within the stone.

Like a flawless diamond with its unique internal fingerprint and characteristics, Jesus is *"THE RADIANCE OF GOD'S GLORY AND THE EXACT REPRESENTATION OF HIS BEING"* (Hebrews 1:3). He shimmers with the character and depth of God's unfailing love. As the jeweler displays a gem on black velvet, God uses disappointment for a dark backdrop to draw our eyes to Jesus. Through His life and how He responds to suffering, God showcases His opulent grace, mercy, kindness, strength, and compassion. Jesus gives us a picture of what it looks like to depend fully on God so we can learn to handle hardship His way. Studying the gospels is like a private showing of God's most precious Stone. He remained obedient in every aspect of His suffering. We can look to His perfect example to learn how to respond when we are lonely, insulted, betrayed, rejected, grief-stricken, and weary. The One who endured and overcame death shows us how to endure our unparalleled faith challenges with invincible courage. He gives us the inextinguishable hope that will never disappoint us. In the many complicated aspects of our situations lay golden opportunities to know God more, as we understand who we are in Christ and learn the necessary skills for handling hardship the way

Jesus did. Face to Face encounters with the Invisible God in His Word lead us to an ever-growing intimacy with Him. Many well-meaning people tried to comfort me by offering reassuring promises that my son would come home. While their words were laced with love, they were void of certainty. God never offers us such frothy optimism. His refreshing honesty about real life and suffering recorded in the pages of Scripture permits us to embrace our own stories of hardship as part of His story of redemption.

The Defining Moment
One visionary picture of God stands out from all the rest. As a new believer, I had more zeal than biblical knowledge. When I read Abraham's story, I believed it meant God planned to spare my son. Each day this passage filled my heart with ecstatic, emotionally charged excitement. A few days later, in the quietness of the morning, I sensed the gentle whisper of God. BETH, WOULD YOU LOVE ME EVEN IF I NEVER BROUGHT YOUR SON HOME? This thought had never entered my mind before. I was confused. To be honest, it terrified me. I fell face down on the floor of my living room and cried out, WHAT ARE

YOU ASKING, LORD? HOW COULD I POSSIBLY ENDURE THE AGONY OF NEVER SEEING MY SON AGAIN?

Has God ever asked you to release something precious into His hands? When grappling with seemingly unbearable challenges in our faith walk, it is vitally important to spend time sitting at the feet of Jesus. When we pour out our doubts, fears, resentments, and failures, He fills our empty hearts with hope. God wants us to share our dark hours, long nights, and deep hurts with Him. When others point fingers, He extends wide-open arms of love. Those same comforting arms will hold us close as we thrash through the distressing spiral of surrendering our wills to God's. Each intense round of hurt anguish, loss, fear, and anger demanded a decision of faith.

Each "yes" to God and "no" to self, can bring the backlash of agonizing emotions, but His divine consolation quiets our terrified hearts. Meditating on the grace and truth of Jesus strengthens our flagging faith by reminding us that He is always with us and fighting for us. The One who endured the most painful experience of all time promises to help us endure ours. In the depths of my soul, I knew I could endure the nightmare of losing my son, provided I had a deep relationship with God's Son, Jesus. I reread the story of Abraham with fresh eyes. "...TAKE YOUR SON, YOUR ONLY SON...WHOM YOU LOVE...SACRIFICE HIM...NOW I KNOW THAT YOU FEAR GOD, BECAUSE YOU HAVE NOT WITHHELD FROM ME YOUR SON, YOUR ONLY SON..." (Genesis 22:1-14).

I LOOKED at Abraham's sacrifice, but this time I SAW God's willingness to sacrifice His Son so this stray child could come home. Rather than excitement, I was awestruck by the love of God. I looked up. FATHER, I KNOW YOU ARE A LOVING GOD. YES, LORD. I WILL STILL LOVE YOU EVEN IF YOU NEVER BRING MY SON HOME. I STILL WANT YOU TO BRING HIM HOME, BUT I WILL LOVE YOU EVEN IF YOU NEVER DO. This sacred moment of surrender launched me into a lifelong lesson of the moment to moment surrendering of myself to the will of my loving God. Faith did not make my disappointment magically disappear. Instead, it gave me the assurance and strength to press on through the uninvited, unexpected, and unavoidable troubles of life. Placing myself and my son into the hands of God changed the focus and trajectory of my life. I began pursuing God instead of chasing after my runaway son. The love of the Invisible God that shimmered on the Cross at Calvary gave me the courage to face my deepest shame, darkest secrets, and terrifying fears instead of hiding behind the self-protective veneer of a perfect life. It changed the way I saw my circumstances. Instead of looking at my son's self-destructive choices, I saw how I was the one who lived as the prodigal who hurt the heart of my Father. Instead of drowning in self-pity, I wept bitterly over the many ways and times I had failed both my son and my Father God. Instead of looking at my failures, I learned to accept and rejoice in God's unfailing mercy and the forgiveness that covers my sin like a heavy blanket of fresh snow.

In the messy, lifelong process of sanctification, I offered the shattered pieces of my life to God; trusting Him to fashion me into a masterpiece that reflects the image of Jesus. Growing up in our faith is hard work. We need to continually decide to make God the Source of everything we need for life and godliness. I do not have a perfect track record, but I worship a perfect God who leads me back whenever I stray.

How to Find the Diamond in Your Disappointment
As believers, our desire shouldn't be to merely go through things, we should want to grow through them. Let me share four key phrases to help us remember that Jesus is the Source of everything we need to outlast all our troubles, no matter how long they last.

1. Go to the Source

Scripture gives us access to the diamond mine of God's flawless wisdom. As the All-wise God, He is the Source of wisdom and urges us to search for it *"AS FOR HIDDEN TREASURE"* (Proverbs 2:4).

Going to the Source of wisdom means first turning to God and searching His Word for the answers to our problems. Trusting God instead of our faulty understanding helps us manoeuvre our way through the dark valleys, keeping us from unnecessary detours into the pit of defeat. Finding the rare jewel of genuine wisdom and living out God's prescribed ways brings the promise of *"RICHES AND HONOR, ENDURING WEALTH AND PROSPERITY"* (Proverbs 8:18).

2. Know the Source

The Bible says, *"THE LORD WOULD SPEAK TO MOSES FACE TO FACE, AS A MAN SPEAKS WITH A FRIEND"* (Exodus 33:11). This infers that Moses had a close and abiding friendship with God. He speaks to us face to face each time we read His written Word. When we lack biblical understanding, our perceptions of God can end up looking more like a distorted caricature of Him. Having a faulty understanding of how God uses trials in the lives of believers can undermine our faith and weaken our confidence. Jesus said, *"NOW THIS IS ETERNAL LIFE: THAT THEY MAY KNOW YOU, THE ONLY TRUE GOD, AND JESUS CHRIST, WHOM YOU HAVE SENT"* (John 17:3). Knowing the real God gives us the courage to face the fiery trials of life.

3. Grow from the Source

"LIKE NEWBORN BABIES, CRAVE PURE SPIRITUAL MILK, SO THAT BY IT YOU MAY GROW UP" (1 PETER 2:2). Digesting the truth can be difficult, especially when we see our failures. But we need to realize these failures can provide valuable information when we pay attention and learn from them. Dealing with hardship God's way means seeking His wisdom about how to handle it and then put it into practice.

In so doing, we develop the skills and abilities we need to persevere through the spiritual growing pains as God matures us. This process of maturity is a gift from God, who wants us to lack for nothing. Never give up! Always continue growing up by continually nourishing your soul on the Word of God.

4.   Glow for the Source

The author of Proverbs writes, *"BY WISDOM A HOUSE IS BUILT, AND THROUGH UNDERSTANDING IT IS ESTABLISHED; THROUGH KNOWLEDGE ITS ROOMS ARE FILLED WITH RARE AND BEAUTIFUL TREASURES"* (Proverbs 24:3-4). Meditating on His Word and aligning our lives with the glittering treasures of His truth are like eating diamonds. It fills our lives with "RARE AND BEAUTIFUL TREASURES" (Proverbs 24:4).

When we persevere in imitating Jesus, His radiant character enables us to glow from the inside out. The One who fed the five thousand continually feeds us with the riches in His Word. We are then to be a blessing to others by sharing those riches of God's Word with others so they too can Go, Know, Grow, and Glow.

A Dazzling Display

One prayer God answered proved to be one of His most dazzling displays of glory as another precious day with my son slipped away. Twilight gave way to darkness as the sun inched its way down the midnight blue sky before sinking beneath the horizon. I leaned down and kissed my sleeping son on the forehead then tip-toed over to the softly lit doorway and stood at the tall wastebasket with my back to his bed as I removed my gloves, mask, and yellow paper gown. Without turning around, I repeated my nightly ritual. I LOVE YOU, SON! At that moment, God broke into the room and splashed His glittering glory over my life. FROM OUT OF THE DARKNESS BEHIND ME, A VOICE BROKE THE EXPECTED SILENCE AND…

About Beth Weber

Beth Weber is a gifted speaker and author with a contagious passion for the Word of God. She is the founder of Hope Services LLC, a speaking organization established to help others persevere and endure hardship with hope. With refreshing transparency, Beth inspires audiences with her compelling stories and practical biblical applications. Watch for the year-end release of her book, The Diamond in Your Disappointment-MINING GOD'S TREASURE IN TRIALS

To schedule Beth to speak at your next event you may contact her by

Mail: P.O. Box 2305 Brighton, MI 48116

Email // bethweberhopes@gmail.com

WWW.BETHWEBERHOPES.COM

SELF TRANSFORMATION TO HEALING

TAYNIA A. MOSLEY

The Start of the Journey

Have you ever been in a desperate search for your husband's love, his friendship, his desire? Have you ever survived a heartbreak? There I was, married to this man for almost ten years of my life with nothing accomplished of my life. My whole 20s was gone. I got married at the tender age of 19 to someone I did not know because our relationship was based upon a lie. He lied to me from the start, but I choose to overlook it all because, by that time, his age didn't matter since I was already madly in love with him, the person I thought he was. Do not get me wrong, we both went through growing pains, changes, and ups and downs, but I had the warning before the marriage, and I ignored the signs.

I grew up in church, so I knew what was right and what was wrong. The moment I decided to have sex, with him, I let him into my heart and began to fall deeper into a hurtful pain. I mean, it was all good at first. It was like we were the best of friends' day in and day out. I knew I was living in sin, and I chose to get married rather than to burn, not knowing that I would burn anyway for jumping the gun and getting married to the wrong man. I had gotten pregnant at 19 and did not want to be looked at or judged for having a baby without being married. We married in February of 2004, and I gave birth at the age of 20 in July 2004 to our first baby girl. Not even two years later, we brought our second baby girl into the world, so much for that boy I never received.

We had a great friendship and an even better love relationship. Then one day something happened, and we never made it back from that. My then-husband lost trust in me and our relationship. He thought I was cheating, but at the time I was not. I was just conversing about much of nothing. He decided not to take my word for it and created a story in his head that he genuinely started to believe. I got a text one day from an old high school friend. He only said good morning, and was catching up on high school days and he told me that he hoped I had a good rest of my day. At the time, I did not think much of it, but to my husband, it meant everything. He began believing that I was hiding things and flirting with every guy from my past. I was always confused about this because if I was not at home with him and our children, I was at work, or running our office cleaning business with him, so I didn't take it too seriously.

I almost instantly noticed a change even though he tried to act like everything was okay. I could tell that he still had his doubts. He began talking to females from his past on social media and then had the nerve to delete me as a friend. I was beyond heated, and although I complained it never made a difference. He would add me back one day and delete me the next. I was over it, so I let it be not knowing that he was blocking me from seeing the interaction on his social media. I had no clue that he connected to so many people (females) from his past. They were bringing back old memories and telling him how much they liked him back then. This gave him the courage to move forward in pursuing relationships he had no business pursuing and he had me all messed up!

I caught him on the phone with the first chick. He was telling her how much he wanted to be with her and how much he was in love with her. Homegirl knew he was married but she didn't care because, as she says, she had fallen in love with him, my husband. I was livid through that phone. I thank God that I had no idea exactly where she was because I would have visited her. It shattered my heart to a million pieces to the cold hard floor. I was crushed and devastated because this came out of nowhere (to me). I did not know how to deal with it. I had not seen anyone I knew personally go through heartbreak with "mistake after mistake."

The Twist

I never felt anything like this in my entire life. I was devastated, hurt, crushed, and bruised. We argued about the situation at hand. I cried, he held me and told me that he would never hurt me again, that it was over. I believed him, so I forgave him. This went on until we divorced. He would straighten up for a few days, weeks, or months, and then it would start all over again. The last time I found out about it was with a different girl who became pregnant not once, but twice by him. On top of all that, one day close to Christmas, he rushed home and needed to borrow some money from me for an "emergency." I later found out that the money was used to pay for an abortion. He used our children's Christmas money to pay for their abortion, and I never got my money back. Talk about depressing; my heart was stomped on so many levels. I had no one to talk too. I mean, really, what would I even say? I felt so lost, embarrassed, and alone. I was not comfortable in my own home with this man who had become someone I no longer knew.

I was too busy being lost from dreaming of what our marriage should have been instead of living in the reality of my failing marriage, which was a total disaster. I believe that when a man and a woman get married, it is for better and/or for worse, rich or for poor, in sickness and in health. Those vows are what people hold on to in the hard and trying times, these vows are a constant reminder of what and who you have committed yourself too. Your vows are what gives life to your marriage. It is our duty to uphold our vows because they were made to our spouses, ourselves, and most of all, to God. Vows are nothing to take lightly. We must hold each other accountable to stay on task, which is to have a life together for the rest of your lives.

I took our vows literally and seriously. I wanted to be the best wife and mother I could be, but it seemed as if the harder I tried, it was never enough. The more I tried, the more he pulled away, making me feel like I was not enough; like I failed at being a good wife and a great mother. I found myself alone a lot, raising our children. It made me ask God how I could be married yet feel like a single parent? I mean, from finances to school, clothes, shoes, etc. it all fell on me because his priority was someplace else. It was like our lives were going back in time because everything he had done, he was no longer doing or even interested in keeping up. The more time went on, I began to cry and weep. I began to call out to God, but I could never hear Him. It seemed like the more I prayed, the emptier the promises had become. I just did not understand because I still was in love with him, even after all of this. I was a complete and total mess. My life was no longer mine; I didn't know me anymore; I could not recognize myself. It was at this point I finally began seeing that our vows meant nothing to him, and they were becoming more distant to me.

The friendship I thought we once shared didn't seem to count for anything. My best friend was long gone, my husband was up for grabs, honey. This marriage was in the worst state for quite some time. It was not the happy ending I had imagined. Our marriage was no fairytale, it was not like the movies, nor was it anything like my parent's union. It had taken a toll on both of our hearts, it changed us. After our second daughter was born, it seemed like all hell had broken loose. Even while pregnant, I felt a great disconnect. It was nowhere near our first pregnancy where he attended every doctor's appointment and was there a lot because I am a high-risk pregnancy (every time).

This second pregnancy was hit or miss without any real excuses. I felt the change, and I am sure our unborn child felt the disconnect. I started to blame myself because even though our baby was coming, she was not planned and we were not ready. I felt like I stepped up to the plate alone. It crushed me like a ton of bricks being dropped repeatedly against my chest. Every time I would believe his lies, his behavior only become more carefree and reckless. There was no truth anymore when we said we loved each other because love would never hurt like this. The fact was I hated him, and most of all, I hated myself for allowing this to go on. I hated myself for becoming bitter and broken while letting hate to fill my heart.

This was not me at all. I grew up believing it is okay to dislike someone, but you should never hate anyone. I always stood by that, and today after being delivered, I still stand by that wholeheartedly. Love is all we need in our hearts because Jesus is love. I was praying that one day our relationship would get better, that he would put me and only me first, and honor and respect our union. There were no changes. I had begun to feel as though I lost my soul.

The light that once shined on the inside of me was gone. I realized my innocence was demolished. I had come out of the church. I felt, what was the point because I had been in church my whole life. I got married, I followed the Bible's principles, I respected my parents, I honored my husband, but I now was left out in the cold, hurt and confused. What did I do wrong? These are the things I kept asking God. Why me? Why do I have to suffer while everyone else is enjoying life? I know it is a cliché, but my answer was simple; God said this is what you wanted, you did not come to me for guidance on if this was the person you were to marry, you did not come to me for advice nor wait for my instruction. This is not my doing daughter; this is all on you because we love to blame God, right? When I finally heard that I felt my knees get weak because He was right. What had I done? He said I have heard your prayers, every one of them, but they are not for this marriage, they are not for this relationship. At that moment I learned to ask God before I did anything. No, it is and was not easy; it is still a learning process, but I have/had to do it.

God's word says in the Holy Bible in Proverbs 3:5-6 to *"Trust in the Lord with all thine heart, and lean not unto thine own understanding. In all thy ways acknowledge him, and he shall direct thy paths."* This scripture is a constant reminder of my past mistakes of not including the Lord into my thoughts, my decisions, and my life.

The Wake-Up Call
In 2010 it all hit me the hardest, I mean I was trying to hold on to this marriage. I almost collapsed there on social media. We were having a great weekend together, so I was saying something about being thankful for my husband taking the girls to the park while I got some rest. Shortly after posting, I got an inbox from this random guy. He said something to the effect of, I'm glad you are happy with him and congratulations on becoming a stepmother. After picking my face up from the ground, I told him that he must have the wrong person. He said no, just ask your husband. He knows exactly what I am talking about. Of course, he denied, denied, denied until one day I could not take it any longer, so I went to go see for myself. The girl only lived around the block from my parents' house; now how embarrassing was that. I knocked on her door and got no answer, so I left a note for her to call me. But instead of calling me, she called to tell him on me. You had to be a fly on the wall, I promise I could not make this up!

This marriage was a living HELL for me. I lost my mind so many times, but God! I thank God for the stranger in my inbox because without him, I probably would have never known. It was all true; about a month after finding out she was pregnant; she went into early labor; there they had the son I always wanted. Another slap in the face. I began to drink heavily until I passed out. I could not take walking around so heavy in my spirit; to not feel the many pieces of my daily heartbreak. I choose to drink my problems away, only to find out that the next day they had gotten even worse. I was in over my head; this was all new to me. I only grew up to see marriages that lasted with love; not perfect marriages, but marriages where they worked the problems out. I could not understand how God allowed me to even get hurt like this. What had I done wrong? For the life of me, I could not figure it out. I knew I had a great work to do internally, so I begin reading spiritual and self-help books instead of the raunchy books I was used too. I tried to fix me because I thought I was the issue.

They say that hurt people go on to hurt other people after so long of this. I found myself becoming my ex-husband. I, too, had started to lie and cheat, whether it was flirting over the phone or going on dates and sometimes having sex; I was deceiving and would leave out important details to keep playing his game. I drank, and I mean, I drank a lot just to keep my body numb, and my heart from feeling any more hurt or emotions.

My heart was now black and bruised. I started taking pain pills to get me through my workday because I did not want to feel disappointment, anguish, or let down from myself. I was inflicting a lot of excess pain upon myself because of this new person I had become. She was not me, the real me. I started to hide things, and I must say that I had gotten surprisingly good at it. He was too busy doing his own thing to ever notice of what I had going on. He was too busy trying to avoid me, and even though I was doing my own thing, I still wanted and needed my husband. I always wanted it to work. I wanted him to choose his family, but he never did. I began to operate out of my brokenness, which was not the right way to function.

Who had I become? I lost the girl I once knew. She was so far gone there was no bringing her back, ever. Shattered daily on the inside from all the lies, fighting, arguing, cheating to fill a void that I could not fill, building relationships with other men, all just to let them down in the end. Even though I was upfront with them, I ended things on my terms, which were very abruptly. Some would classify it as a one-night stand, but I just decided to keep it moving. There were not many, but there were multiple because I was looking for something that could not be found.

No, matter how hard I tried, or they tried, they just were not what I wanted, desired, or needed. Having someone else was never enough for me, it did not satisfy my soul. My soul yearned for more than just random sex. It was crying out for attention from a man who was nowhere in sight. I mean, yes, we lived together but the connection had been lost a long time ago. We barely even touched each other. Although we still handled business, laughed, and joked from time to time, the flame was out.

It is not my intent to make my ex-husband out as the bad guy because the truth is, we both were wrong; we were not ready for what was in store for us. This is just a story from my point of view, from my brokenness into my healing transformation. Although it took me some time to get through all this misplaced trust, resentment, rejection, bitterness, hatred, and pain, it was not all on him. I fought him too, I yelled and screamed at him too, I cheated too, and I also lied. If I can be honest, looking back I had no clue what my role was as a wife because I instantly became the weaker one in our marriage. I allowed him to cause me to think I had done something wrong, but in actuality, it was him in the beginning. I let him live a lie as if he did not have a family at home. I was his wife, but I felt more like the side chick in the life we lived.

Transformation
It had not fully hit me until 2012 after fasting and continuously praying; God told me that he was not going to change, to file for a divorce, and to let it go. To me, this sounded like run girl run, lol so that is what I did. I started researching how to file for a divorce in my state, and I served him. I watched him get served right in our front room as I packed to go out of town for a couple of days with my family. It was a total shock to him because, let us be honest, how many times had I said that I was done with this marriage because I had been hurt too many times to even count. What a waste of time, what a waste of my youthful years some would say, but I call it a blessing because I learned so much about myself.

In Psalm 103:5 NLT, it says *He fills my life with good things. My youth is renewed like the eagles!* God restored my soul after everything was said and done because I had become a complete savage. I was truly heartless and cold.
My heart could not take any more pain, and there I was stuck, glued to my bed. The day after my divorce was finalized it finally hit me that after ten whole years, I was no longer a wife. I was no longer tied down to an unfaithful marriage, an unfaithful husband, or a deceitful life. I was tired of trying because it seemed as if no matter how hard I tried, it just would not work.

I later realized that it was not designed for me to do it all on my own. It should have been the both of us working on our marriage, but it was just me. So yes, I was finally happy to no longer be bound to a dark depression, stuck inside of a relationship where I was not wanted. There was no longer a dark cloud hanging over my head every day. I no longer searched to fill a void that was unfillable because I genuinely desired my husband and our marriage, but it was time to let it go. It was just my children and me, and I was starting to be okay with that. I needed to get to know me, the new me, and what I liked, desired, and needed.

Even though I was finally starting to feel happy, I was still sad at the same time because I had failed at being a wife, a friend, and a confidant. The sadness did not go away overnight. I had to rededicate my life back to the Lord. I had to get rebaptized to get set free from the spirit of brokenness. I felt the Lord closer to me again, I knew that everything was going according to His divine will for my life. I trusted God and depended on Him because all else had failed me. I needed the Holy Spirit like I needed my next breath to stay free, to become happy again for the possibilities of love. So many people walk around hurting because they do not want to forgive, or they do not know how to truly forgive, let go, and move on.

When thinking about forgiveness, one must understand that forgiving a person is not for that person, it is for yourself. It is to set yourself free from the bondage of hurting by holding on to bad past experiences. There is no need to be 45 and still mad at something that happened when you were 23. It just doesn't make sense to hurt yourself for that long because trust me, the person that has done you wrong has moved on while you are still stuck in the past, thinking of the tragedy day in and day out. Unforgiveness is not a right place to be in. I had the opposite problem. I repeatedly forgave myself for the same offense, not to mention I gave in way too fast because I wanted my marriage to work. I thought this is what it took to forgive and move on from the cheating, the lies, the fights, and the mental abuse, but it seemed as though I was the only one who moved on, for the moment anyway.

I forgot that I was my most prized possession and that if I did not look out for myself, no one else ever will. That was something I had to learn the hard way. I wanted my husband to be my protector, my friend, the one whom I could trust with my life, but time again I learned that I only had me, myself, and I. I believe age had a lot to do with it, but I would say that for the most part, the maturity level is what stomped us out. We were young when we got married, I was 19 and pregnant, he was 18; but what trips me out the most is the first three years were magical. That is why I can say that yes, we were young, but it was more than our missing growth as a couple. I mean yeah, we grew together, but as time went on, we became more apart than we were together.

The most important thing is knowing when it is time to make a change. Deciding to better yourself, to better your life, and if you have children, it is to better yourself for your children. You must begin loving yourself unconditionally because no one is perfect. We all make mistakes, but we must get back up to face ourselves. We cannot keep bumping our heads on the same spot and expect to receive healing on that wound. Even if you have no clue how or what it will take for your transformation, you still must decide. Pray to God because He will direct your path, He will give you directions concerning the situation; just talk to Him. Pour out your heart and cleanse your soul to get your breakthrough and your healing because it is yours. Forgiveness starts with self; we must learn to forgive ourselves from the past mistakes. Some things we created and some things we allowed to happen to us.

Of course, there are times when we had no control over the situation, but we still blame ourselves for it happening. It is not your fault, please, I beg of you to let yourself off the hook and forgive. Forgiveness takes a lot of work, and I am not telling you it is easy, but it is necessary to cleanse your heart. Once you have forgiven yourself, it is time to forgive those who have wronged you. Say a prayer and ask the Lord to show you how to forgive, and I mean really forgive and let the offense go. As women, we tend to hold onto things that no longer serve us because we have not figured out how to truly let a situation go. Yes, it happened to you, but it does not define the rest of your life. It should not and cannot dictate your future. The more thought you give a situation, the more power that situation has over you.

The Holy Bible says in Ephesians 4:26-27, "*Be ye angry, and sin not: let not the sun go down upon your wrath: Neither give place to the devil.*" Remember, "He who angers you controls you." Never give your power to people, especially those who mean you no good. It is a conscious choice and a conscious decision to forgive, to not dwell in the past, to not remain stuck in the past.

To be able to move on and free your heart, the first step is to forgive all parties, including yourself. Drop the charges as my pastors would say, pray about the situation, pray for the situation, let the tears flow, give it to God and leave it there. It is time to work on a better you, starting right here and right now. No more excuses; it is time to face yourself in the mirror, and like Michael Jackson says, make that change starting with the man in the mirror. Just because you forgive a person does not mean you must let that person back into your life the way they once were. It just means that you forgive them, and you are letting the situation go. It does not mean trust comes back automatically, that will take work. Forgiveness is to free you as the person holding everything on the inside of you; it is to give you a release, a cleansing, a renewal, inner strength, and healing.

Once you learn to forgive and move past the situation, you can start to focus on yourself more and the things you will need to do to become a better version of yourself. How can you continuously pour from an empty cup or an empty version of yourself? Most times we must stop everything and give ourselves time for self-care to self-heal. We must take time to feed our souls and heal our wounds. This is not an overnight process, but continuous work every single day of our lives. Each day, week, or month carve out some time in your schedule to focus on you. Do an emotional self-check with yourself, write out your feelings, pray about it, and give it all to God. If it is too much for you to handle by yourself, get yourself a coach and/or a therapist because you need to release the negative feelings to shift into a positive state of mind. Heal from the inside and transform your life. It will be the best thing you can do for yourself to heal your emotions.

The first three years of our marriage were fun and exciting, but then I guess you can say real life happened, and baby when I say real life happened, I don't believe either one of us was ready for what came our way. We were married for a total of ten years, where only the first three were of some value. I am glad to say that three months before my 30th birthday, I gained my independence back. I was finally free and divorced, but with that I had to go deep within to do some much-needed work. I needed to find the new me because I was broken. With God on my side, I was able to coach myself into my destiny, where I birthed out *Destined With A Purpose* relationship and spiritual self-help and devotional books and coaching.

About
Taynia A. Mosley

Spiritual and Relationship Coach. I Am Destined With A Purpose!

Taynia A. (Coleman) Mosley is a Relationship Coach and the author of *An Unnecessary Breakdown Within Your Relationship: Communication Is Key*, who helps broken hearted people whether married, engaged, single, or dating become unstuck in their love walk. By helping them heal and to be completely made whole again with forgiveness and love for others. To start the healing process, you must decide to become whole again, to love, and to forgive yourself so you can love and forgive others. It is imperative to love thyself without a doubt.

Before starting Destined With A Purpose, and after successful career in helping people solve everyday life issues, writing a self-help book helping people to navigate through relationships and communication matters became her life focus. Going through a bad marriage/divorce is where her work started. Through experience and her faith in God, she began relationship coaching through helping other broken people become unstuck and live again. Taynia now coaches people on how to show up for themselves to

show up inside of their relationship for others. She also offers spiritual meditation sessions where she works on the inner man by self-healing to learn how to cleanse your mind, soul, body, and spirit through different techniques.

Taynia is available for all your spiritual and relationship coaching needs, which includes private consultations sessions as well.

FACEBOOK: IAMDESTINEDWITHPURPOSE | IG: TAYNIAMOSLEY
TWITTER: TAYNIAMOSLEY

(248) 403-0724 | destinedwithapurposellc@gmail.com

www.destinedwithpurpose.com

HE'S BIGGER THAN MY MISTAKES

SARAH WILLIAMS

I know the thoughts that I think toward you, Says the Lord, Thoughts of peace and not evil, To give you a future and a hope. (Jeremiah 29:11 NKJV)

My early childhood years were wonderful. Being the only girl sibling and having much of what I wanted; dolls and pretty clothes, faithful loving parents, and both sets of grandparents. I was "made over" by everyone, feeling as though I was "kind of special" if you will. In short, I enjoyed being a smart, obedient, pretty little girl. Further solidifying my feeling special, I was always hearing, "I was dark skin and pretty," I was proud to be a good representation for myself and my family. Helping people has always been a part of me; being a nurse or missionary were early aspirations. A loving little church girl with a vivid imagination, but then suddenly things began to change.

Hello Adolescence. This particular day, I could not have imagined. It was a wet, gray Wednesday evening, not like my typical favorite day of the week. Exhausting all efforts to stay calm, thinking how it will be over soon. I didn't know what to expect. "My mother knows what to do; she always protects me from any hurt or trouble." So here we are, on the way to see this doctor, "Dr. Quack."

After leaving the tall office building on Woodward Ave. with an eerie and weird feeling, I am now trying to digest the bad news that he could not help me. I don't remember very much about our journey home, only sitting in the car with an awkward silence between my mother and me. It was a scene of something final. She began to cry. I had never heard that sound from her before. Feeling down and troubled, I had a deep and unexplained sadness. "Oh God, What now!" Seeing my mother fall apart was devastating, I knew she was hurting not only for me, but herself as well. It was a painfully numbing experience.

Upon entering the house, the encouraging words offered by my oldest brother made it seem as if everything was going to be alright. It was not the end of the world, but it sure felt like the end of my world. It was not just a change in my world. It is hard to understand that your decisions are not just about you, they also affect others. The trickling effect of decisions can be decisively positive or negative, requiring sacrifices in many lives. Indeed, this kind of knowing does not come easy. It comes with maturity.

The Core
It really all started last year, October. Sweet Sixteen! Happy Birthday to me! It wasn't quite my expectation or dream. There was no Debutante Ball or a big celebration. As a matter of fact, I did not know anyone who had a Sweet 16 bash. It was what I wanted, something formal and special when I arrived at this age. You hear how this is a turning point in the life of a teen. My story unfolds like one I had never heard.

It began on a Friday evening. I had gone shopping for a new outfit, got my first Afro haircut at D's Barber Shop, and all of this was funded by him. Gearing up to get picked up by a man twice my age, exactly the plan I didn't know. Staying out late won't be a problem because Mama will be working her midnight shift, which gives me plenty of room to maneuver.
I am all ready for my first date with him. I say date because the brief prior meeting in his car when he paid me was just a meeting. This was somewhat different. I was inquisitive, with no apprehension; I was gamed as they would say.

After arriving in his pretty new car, we rode around a while, got a take-out Bar-B-Q dinner, and ended up at the Motel 8 Inn. I suppose you could say I had tested the waters before, but nothing as deep as this. Spending the night with him gave me a different kind of emotion. I would think about it for days to come. What is this?

We met while I was standing at the bus stop in front of his business. I was introduced to him by a schoolmate who was his employee. Being a man of means and power, I guess, was the initial attraction. It's not like he was so "fine." Ironically, I was now yearning for a feeling I could not explain.

Fall season turned into winter, and I was relishing in my secret affair. Then my mother found out about my antics of sneaking him in and out of the house. Really! Frequenting motels became more complicated, with the responsibility of caring for my younger brothers and the house while Mama was working. Feeling grown enough to do what I wanted, I found myself caught up into something I knew nothing about. I could even quit school legally. Identifying with the broken home statistic that teenagers act out, somehow, I felt justified.

The cold, snowy winter was exciting for me as I did whatever was necessary to continue in this forbidden affair. It did not make me feel proud. On the one hand, I wanted to stop. My mother did all she could to dissolve my immature bad choices. I am sure her feelings of despair must have been overwhelmingness matched with helplessness, especially after hearing the disappointing news from the legal authorities that her 16-year-old was now at "The Age of Consent." The weight of the tension on our great relationship proved to be heavy to bear.

After a disquieting winter of sneaking and experimenting, the summer finally arrived. It was fun, fast, and disturbing. There were not many activities for a man to do with an underage girl. We spent lots of time doing outdoor things, and I also learned to drive. Riding around from county to county was a daily activity, loitering at fast-food spots, settling in areas where he was the most popular. Yes, many people saw but no one said much, not where you could hear anyway. Evidently, I was not the first young girl he brought around to "showboat." The truth is, I did not really give it that much thought. A couple of my friends would always hang out with us, going on outings to the parks where we always felt free. Visiting his friends in the next state over was just one more grown up thing to do. Just a fresh, green young girl acting out and pretending to be in a "semi-adult state of mind."

One very hot day, the four of us were riding around enjoying the weather, having fun, and doing new and different things. I had not been feeling my best that day, but now, for some reason, I was really sick. I began vomiting, which made me feel even more miserable. I tried to get it together after a bit, but it just was not happening. I could not wait to get home.

There was no place like the comfort and security of home. The awkwardness of living this edgy lifestyle as a sixteen-year-old was becoming somewhat of a burden. It had me confused. The desire was still there to keep going, but now it seemed taboo, as I asked myself how do I move on? There was a hold on me that I did not understand. The stress between my mother and I seemed to have eased up a bit. She tried to use her strategy to make this grown "intruder" disappear" It was a lot to deal with, and I was getting more uncomfortable with the whole scene as time went by. He stole my innocence. I was raped with consent. I learned much later there was a name for that kind of behavior; saying yes, not knowing that I was being taken advantage of by an adult male.

What would cause me to choose this way? Was it a response to the brokenness I suffered from a recent split home, could it be the allure of wanting to grow up too fast, or was it the freedom that I was privileged to have from being raised by a single responsible parent who was doing everything she could just to provide for our basic needs? Through the whole process, I felt alone.

Dear Mama, I began my five-page letter apologizing to my mother for the stress and disappointment I had caused her the prior year. Coming out of the fog, I began seeing things more clearly. I no longer wanted to be a part of this escapade that I had chosen. It had been a whirlwind of a year but now it was time for school to begin. I was ready to get back on the right track and act like the young lady I was expected to be. As I wrote my heartfelt words to my mother, my heart became heavy. Unfortunately, it's too late for the damage is done. I was glad to be able to share my thoughts and feelings, but they should have come earlier. We now have a more permanent problem.

Talking to God, I was scolding myself and asking the famous question, "Why Me?" This didn't happen to any of the others who were in my circle of friends, and in my opinion, we all were doing things we shouldn't have been doing at that tender age. There was so much more to be expected, I could not handle this new reality. There was a conscious moment when I felt abandoned by God. Why didn't he save me from that pain? Did I think for one moment that my actions were not going to lead to something permanent? I knew about the possibility of getting knocked up, but it definitely was not at the forefront of my thoughts. Now it is a fact that I was sneaking around, participating in wrong behavior; but a lot of my dismay came because it was with a grown man.

It is funny how we do those things in the dark that we do not want to be seen in the light. That light made my life awful, more so than when my parents separated. There were such depression and a cloud of shame that I carried it from room to room wherever I went. I stopped seeing everyone, except for my immediate family.

I occasionally went with mom to the grocery store, and of course, visiting my grandmother on my mother's side and I hated it! I was starting to poke out a little. My grandmother unknowingly tried not to look at me. As I continued making it through the hardest few months of my young life, the burden was lifted for some unknown reason when the birth came two months early. I was a happy camper. The experience was unexplainable! I had no idea what to expect. I had not been able to attend any classes or read any books to prepare me for giving birth and being a new mother. All I heard is that it was going to hurt. Well, I got through that, and now I'm feeling somewhat free. Maybe I can live a little.

Although some of the pressure has been lifted from me, I was now starting to feel the stigma of being a seventeen-year-old teenage mother who just had a baby out of wedlock. There was no real happiness for the birth of my child except by his father. I could only assume it was because of his ego and ignorance. It did not make any sense otherwise as to why he would feel proud at his achievement. Mothers will always be mothers, and of course, mine did her best to make me feel fine and get me through all this.

I was having a major problem that made my new role of motherhood difficult. I felt I was not connecting with my baby. Finances were not the problem, but adjusting spiritually into motherhood, and emotionally being affectionate to my baby was. I loved my child, but it was also a reality that I didn't want to be in this position at my age, so I believe that I carried a sense of rejection for my child. I was trying to figure all this out. No one blatantly said to me any of the things that I perceived; maybe it was because I thought my family was disappointed in me.

Could it have been the "she said he said" I had heard? Whatever the reason, I internalized a lot of negative perceptions. I knew I needed to get back on the right track. I went back to school, taking night classes to get my high school diploma. I thought I was too grown to go back to my high school, especially being a grade behind. Then someone told me about the possibility of getting a GED certificate instead of a diploma. I had never heard of anything like that. It was so exciting to discover that I had options. That was my motivation.

Turning eighteen, my mother gave me a pep talk. "Time to start paying your way as an adult. You're now eighteen years old, a mother, and a grown woman in every way," that's how she explained it to me. So, I did. I will say this ended up being good for me, because it taught me a lesson of responsibility. I received some aid from the state for a brief period, but I thought I was too good for that. Not much was mentioned about getting a job, just going to school.

Trying to stay focused on moving ahead, I connected with a young man from the old neighborhood. He was very nice to my child and me; unfortunately, he also was in the business of selling drugs, therefore what I needed for money was not an issue. I began feeling somewhat better, coming up from that attitude of semi depression.

My relationship with him allowed me to do a couple of things. I was able to keep some money in my pocket, enabling me to do things for my mother, look out for friends, buy lots of clothes, and once again go about doing things my way, Yet, I still was not at the place where I wanted to be. I didn't really want to deal with the drug scene drama. The negative world of drugs was not a life that I desired. I still felt as if I did not choose this life but was instead forced into the place where I had now come to live.

It was a gradual process, but I started seeing life in a bit more positive light. I was no longer fighting the gloom as much, instead I was just trying to get through it because some things you just cannot change. Marriage and children were not on my mind, instead my thoughts were of going to college in California, then having a career in the movie and entertainment industry and eventually living a jet-set lifestyle. These dreams made me feel good, but it seemed I was so far from that becoming a reality, and I had no idea how I would get there.

A lot happened in a short period. It was a spontaneous trip. When the question was asked, "Do you want to go," I immediately said, yes! Within a few hours, I was on an airplane for the first time on my way to Los Angeles, California. The trip happened so quick that we did not even bring any luggage. After checking into our hotel, we went shopping for clothes. Here I was, standing on Sunset Blvd. I knew at that moment that this was the place for me. My relationship with my very nice boyfriend afforded me a few memorable experiences. Unfortunately, our getaway abruptly ended prematurely. I had to hurry back home because my mother was having emergency surgery.

Looking back at that trip now, I learned much. Oh, how I wished I could have stayed longer. It was beautiful and exciting, but I was not in the most respected company. My fabulous trip was interrupted for reasons I may never fully understand. I do know that the spirit of God allows our direction to be altered at times for our betterment. I am a firm believer that God takes what appears to be bad, and somehow because of his grace and mercy uses it to further our progress.

Masking my discomfort, I blossomed in other areas. I began socializing more in the company of my boyfriend's environment. I continued having mixed emotions. One evening the two of us were at a house of ill repute, you might say, when two of my girlfriends unexpectedly showed up. We had not seen each other in quite a while. They located me after going by the house and visiting my mother. We were elated to see each other and immediately decided to go see a play at the Vest Pocket theatre.

We had so much fun. I still can remember the orange and black ensemble that I was wearing. We were late and giggly, having smoked some weed before we got there. It was the last night of the show's run. Seating was limited, so luckily, we didn't draw too much attention. I still laugh about that night. I was approached by one of the actors who just so happened wasn't performing on that night. He asked me an out of the blue question, "What do you want to do?" From that introduction, a few weeks later and with a little maneuvering from my girlfriends, we began a relationship.

Soul Alteration
In God's omniscience, he had something in store that would change me from a negative to a positive. Of course, at the time I felt confused and lost and, most of all, with a cloud of shame over my head, I was not aware of and/or understood HIS unconditional love for me. I was looking at the world from only one perspective, my own. I carried my negative experience within, not realizing that I had a choice to see things differently.

The time came, and I made that choice. It was a new day, a new attitude. Something different was happening in me. The sunshine was brought into my life. It was exciting and inspirational, a completely different environment than the previous ones I had been associated with. This provided the motivation I needed to dismiss a relationship with my drug dealer boyfriend and all that came along with it. I knew he cared for me, but it was time to move on. I was not content in that place anyway. I just was going along in the meantime, but God heard my plea, my cry, and my silent moans.

"The Lord has heard my supplication; the Lord will receive my prayer." (Psalm 6:9)

Meeting someone with a more positive outlook was great. Those next few months moved at a fast pace. As they say: "Time flies when you're having fun." Our time together was drawing to an end because he was just in town on tour, and he was preparing to go back home. It was a good relationship for me, even if only lasted for a couple of months. I began thinking more seriously about what I really wanted to do, and how to have a different outlook on motherhood. It was sort of sad as he prepared to leave. Somehow, I believed that we would still remain friends. One day as we were having a conversation, he unassumingly asked, "Why don't you come back with me?"

My initial reaction was to blow it off, but as the days went by it became more of serious consideration. As I pondered it, this seemed more like a dream. How I wish, I thought, but I have my baby. Plus, I really didn't know him that well. That, and all the other variables as to why I just could not get up and leave and go across the country, "depending on a stranger" to a place I desired.

After speaking to my mother and her positive attitude regarding the idea, I started thinking maybe this is possible. My mother thought my friend was a gentleman and had the qualities of a good man. She agreed to keep my child while I went with him and reached for something better. Then, after getting settled, I would come back and get my child.

You can't imagine how wonderful I was feeling. Can this really be happening? Do things really happen this way in this day and age? How did this person appear in my life for the good and want to help me realize a dream without really knowing me? Only God could have set this up, that same God I believed had forgotten about me. Everything is now falling right into place. I completed the requirements for my high school diploma, so I was ready to attend college out West, get my hand into some acting, and entertainment. All of a sudden, this was presented to me, and it was real.

A few months after my friend left and returned to California, I eagerly got everything together to leave home. It was a dream come true. Unlike my previous trip to the golden state, this time I was on the plane with lots of luggage and boxes, and my little typewriter, flying to Oakland. I arrived and was warmly greeted by everyone. He was everything that he presented himself to be a good, honest guy. It took a few changes, but I eventually moved to Los Angeles where I experienced a world that I had only dreamed of. I was so grateful, and I came returned to Detroit much sooner than planned to get my child.

Living and learning, there were still ups and downs. I began my journey to diligently seek the Lord. Who is this God? Now I can see that my path was re-directed not just for my fulfillment, but for me to reach a position of commitment to live a holy life, to follow his word. Only God knew how I felt within. Thank God that whatever negative feelings and thoughts I was hearing in one ear; in the other ear there was always his quiet voice, keeping me, and helping me to hold on. I did not want the life that was presented to me, seemingly a life I did not choose. That was my issue with God; I did not choose this. At the time, I didn't understand God's "gift" of free will.

The results of our choices bring either joy or pain. One must take responsibility for which path they choose to travel on. Action, reaction, deed, consequences, seed, harvest. There is no need for self-punishment or constant ridicule. These things only bring your spirit down and distracts your focus from moving forward. Tools of stagnation are guilt, shame, anger, or regret, and these can lead to a place of depression.

"...He was wounded for our transgressions...the punishment fell on him. (Isaiah 53:4-5)

God's love, the "Redeemer" always gives us a choice. Something better is still available. Do not submit to a spirit that keeps you in a negative view of yourself. No matter what the struggle could possibly be, if you're down, you can come up. While you may be in an unhealthy place, you do not have to remain there.

"The Lord is near to those who have a broken heart and saves such as have a contrite spirit. Many are the afflictions of the righteous, but the Lord delivers him out of them all." (Psalm 34:17-18)

Regardless of what persuades the mindset of feeling less than "up to par," whatever the pressure from the expectations of others may put on you, it's what you except about yourself that plays the major part. See yourself as God sees you. You do not need to carry hardship, place to place, time upon time. You really can lay your burden down and leave it there.

I learned early on to keep my business and my emotions to myself, like many of us do. If I had only known at the time that there was another young lady with a similar experience, and that I had not been punished by the Almighty, so there was no need to hide my real pain, I wouldn't have needed to feel so alone. We want our decision to be made not from a place of pain but from a place of transformation.

Many times, I have thought, "if this or that" had not happened, there would have been less grievance for me, but my journey is my journey. I know that knowledge is power, and knowledge in the word of God is strength. To know better is to do better. Amen.

The sacrifice on the cross represents all, and everything. We are never alone. *"Be strong and of good courage, do not fear nor be afraid of them, the Lord your God, He is the one who goes with you. He will never forsake you"* (Deuteronomy 31:6 NKJV). There is no place for self-condemnation. He forgave you, therefore you can forgive yourself. *"I write to you little children, because your sins are forgiven you for his names sake"* (Psalm 103:10-11 NKJV).Life is not made up of burdens, but of lessons learned through adverse situations to reveal to us that there is a God, a "perfect spirit" that resonates in the earth for our growth and our good.

"But may the God of all grace who called us to his eternal glory by Christ Jesus, after you have suffered a while, perfect, establish strengthen and settle you." (1 Peter 5:10 NKJV)

I have experienced much, and I thank God that I have learned much. I have learned firsthand the truth of Luke 7:47 (NKJV). *"Therefore I say to you, her sins, which are many, are forgiven, for she loved much. But to whom little is forgiven, the same loves little."* It's a joy to be able to share inspired words and revelations of life's lessons. My book of prayers and inspirations *Simply Words, Reaches the Ears of Heaven* will soon be available.

SaLou'

About
Sarah Williams

Sarah Williams is a native of Detroit, Michigan, mother of one son, two daughters, and a grandmother of eight. Music is my first passion. She has shared her gifted voice as a soloist with several local gospel groups spreading the good news.

Sarah is now able to share her passion for writing in hopes of encouraging and inspiring someone to know God's Love in their daily experiences. Sarah is a member of Scott Memorial United Methodist Church: Rev. Cornelius Davis Jr. She is also a Certified Lay Servant committed to Evangelism, Prayer, and Performing Arts ministries.

SaLou' Productions Intimate Events and More
(248) 308-6460 | slprod1@yahoo.com
PO Box 90178 Redford, MI, 48239

SAVED JUNKIE

DR. TARESA MOORE

How did I get here?

I was in the middle of my living room floor, crying uncontrollably. My head was spinning, and I was at a total loss for words. *How long was I going to keep persecuting God's people? How long was I going to keep simply existing?* These were the hard questions I had to ask myself as I was having a Saul/Paul moment. I was literally experiencing a panoramic view of my past 37 years, and what I saw was *not pretty!* I needed a radical mind-shift; more importantly, I needed to be delivered.

Anger and selfishness were the strongholds that prevented me from healing. Because of this, my lifestyle was in jeopardy. I had to restructure my mindset for it was detrimental to my survival. On January 24, 1973, I came bursting onto the scene. I was born to a pair of complex individuals in an era when drugs were the norm. As a result of frequent drug use, I was a crack-addicted baby, weighing only three pounds at birth. Doctors told my parents that I had little to no chance of survival. Thirty-seven years later, I was still living in the shadows of that grim prognosis. I saw myself as this grown, crack-addicted baby who was abandoned, rejected, and unloved. Of course, I had grown in stature and age; yet I was still the little girl who was craving something that only God could give me.

I always needed *something*. That something was the love and acceptance of my parents. I wanted to feel something, anything, as a sign that I was not a mistake. I wanted to know that I was loved. This could be the reason why I stayed high on marijuana or alcohol. It provided a temporary euphoria. I liked the way I felt when I was high. I was floating and free in the moment. But those feelings never lasted long enough; I always wanted more. What I needed was vastly different from what my flesh craved. My flesh wanted the quick fixes, but I needed a permanent change—a remedy that man could not give me.

I accepted Jesus at an early age, and I read about Him. My grandmother testified of His goodness, but I had no clue who He was. Where was this Jesus? It was not until March 12, 2010, when I had a divine encounter. I realized that I was loved and accepted by God. This is the day that my deliverance began. God showed me in His Word that He loved me so much that He gave His only child as a ransom for me so that I could live an abundant life. This literally changed my world when I thought about how loving God had to be to find me special enough to sacrifice His Son for me. Oh, what love that is! This was the love I had been longing for all my life: an endless love. This love was coming from someone who owed me nothing yet gave me everything.

Proverbs 23:7 says, "As a man thinks in his heart, so is he." My thoughts, at the time, reflected that of a poverty mindset. It's no secret that I grew up in a poverty-stricken area. Money was tight, and I had a "by any means necessary" attitude. Most days, I lived in the moment; I could not be concerned with the cares of the next day. In fact, I carried that attitude for most of my life. Regardless, if I had to sell drugs, use my body, or if it meant dating a drug dealer, I did whatever was necessary to survive. When my mother was around, she worked a low-paying job. Food was scarce and money was invincible.

My hierarchy of needs were shelter and food. So, it is safe to assume that I damaged my credit at an early age. I had little regard for paying bills outside of the necessary ones, rent, car note, and insurance. Everything else went into a hat, and whatever funds were left went toward what I pulled out of the hat that week. It was not until I looked in God's Word for a direction that my mindset changed. As a servant, God wanted me to be a good steward over my temple and the resources He had given me.

Deliverance means to release anything that holds you captive. God wants us to be free. He never intended for us to be held in bondage by anything or anyone. As a believer, I had been granted the right to command the day and declare that I was free from everything that conflicted with the Word of God. This sounds good; however, this process was complicated for me. I didn't know what this looked like until God showed me.

It started with my *mind*. The lenses through which I viewed myself were totally different from the way God saw me. Psalm 139:14 (MSG) says, *"body and soul, I am marvelously made,"* yet, I saw myself as a failure. Because I had a poverty mindset, I could not see beyond my childhood conditions, even though I was an adult. In my mind, I was in survival mode. I pushed myself beyond my limits to ensure I would never be in poverty again. I thought if I worked hard enough, made enough money, and owned all the right things, life would be grand. Life was not grand for me. In fact, I was living a nightmare—until God rescued me. This came when I surrendered and emptied myself to the Lord.

Once I purged myself and got off the floor, the real work began. I was a believer, and I knew God was a helper. I just wasn't sure that He would help *me*. Sounds crazy, right? Sure, I had heard about and even witnessed the power of God working in the lives of others. But I needed Him to do this for me. I couldn't do this by myself! I needed help, so I prayed. Opening my mouth to talk to God was easy. I spoke the Word over my mind. When thoughts surfaced that did not line up with the Word of God, I spoke to those thoughts. Next, I opened my Bible and looked up every Scripture pertaining to thoughts. I wrote them down and grabbed ahold of 2 Corinthians 10:5, which encourages the believer to cast down imaginations and every high thing that exalts itself against the knowledge of God. This was a revelatory moment for me because I understood that, through this Word, things were going to try to exalt themselves in my thoughts. I had the authority to cast them down. So, that is exactly what I did. I took authority over the things I allowed to enter my mind by using the Word of God. This did not happen all at once. I had to go through the process. Deliverance is necessary. Breaking free from bondage allows us to live authentically, the way God intended for His children to live. We cannot completely fulfill our assignments if we're in bondage. I couldn't enjoy life because I was constantly adding things to my daily schedule to help me avoid the reality of my unhappiness. But no matter how many items I added to the list, I was never satisfied.

Regardless of the many positions I held, the money I made, or the accolades I received from others, nothing was ever enough until I invited Jesus to fill the void. I rededicated my life to God. I was saved, but I felt the need to confess with my mouth and believe in my heart again that Jesus was the Son of God. It was in the opening of my heart to God that I felt a sense of His presence, and I started to trust Him. Through the reading of the Word, I began to see myself. The words became alive in me! For the first time in my life, I experienced clarity of thought. I was no longer double minded and unstable, giving me new meaning to the statement by former slave trader John Newton, "I was once blind, but now I can see." God removed the tinted glasses I was used to donning and replaced them with His mindset. I was wonderfully made with precision and thought, I no longer needed to be a prisoner of my way of thinking. My mind was free, and I was on the path to living with purpose.

Surrendering plays a major role in deliverance. Anything we make bigger than God will rule us. I desired to move forward and be happy, but my inner self was stubborn and had issues yielding to authority. I lived for so many years with the hurt, pain, and rejection that it had become a safety blanket. These emotions were mine, and no one was going to take them from me. I was in charge of living life the way I wanted to. My heart was hardened, and God was the only one who could soften it. This finally happened when I was totally over *me*, and I lifted my hands. I had enough of the lip service, the slinky techniques, and the lies. I was over *me*. I finally said, "I quit!" At that moment, help came in like a torrential flood. God led me to read Ephesians. It was within those pages I learned and accepted that I was chosen before the foundation of the world. God chose me, and I have a purpose. Although I was broken, I had a true identity in Christ. I was declared "Not Guilty!" and set free from sin. I no longer had to hold others hostage; I needed to forgive others as Christ forgave me. I thank God for allowing me to apologize to my mother. This enabled us to establish a relationship, and an unbreakable bond was formed. God totally removed the pain and rejection once I surrendered. All things were made new. My mindset and heart were renewed. I was free to love wholeheartedly, and I honored my mother until the day she took her last breath on January 27, 2014.

Releasing people was one of the most challenging things I had to do in the deliverance process. I needed to loosen the grip on the people who scarred me, but I did not want to. I wanted them to feel the same pain and hurt I did. God's Word pricked my heart in this area. The Bible specifically tells us that vengeance is the Lord's. Even with this, I wanted to be the judge, jury, and executioner. I wanted to inflict the same gut-wrenching, mind-debilitating agony that I felt on my parents. I knew that I loved them, yet I hated them at the same time. Then, I read the Word of God and stumbled upon this verse. *"As Christ is, so are we"* (2 Corinthians 10:7). Wow! All this time, I was looking at my parents as the problem when God was wanting me to take a look in the mirror.

Since I am the reflection of Christ, I needed to release myself before I could release others. The lightbulb finally went off. I was led to seek help from a mental health therapist to address some of my self-sabotaging behavior and blame that I could not release on my own. Therapy helped me tremendously, along with the Word of God. But I had to do the work.

The Lord was requiring me to not only read His Word, but to grab ahold and make the Word my lifestyle. It was in my reading of the Word of God that I was able to fully understand that my beginning did not dictate my ending. I also discovered that, since I received and believed the Lord Jesus Christ, I was given the power to become a son (woman) of God. I was family; I was no longer abandoned or rejected. I was a member of the royal priesthood.

Receiving love from others was extremely difficult for me. I didn't have the opportunity to experience a close-knit, loving relationship with my father. So naturally, receiving love from a man was a strange concept to me. The encounters I had with my father were not favorable as a child; therefore, I had nothing to compare a loving relationship to, unfortunately. My earliest recollection was my parents leaving me with a neighbor who later became my Godmother. The next recollection was my parents separating. Life was never the same for me again. The man who was supposed to love and protect me now abandoned me once again. My life was chaotic. This caused me to always strive to overachieve, which began early on in my childhood. I am still an overachiever today. I never expressed my feelings; instead, I blocked them all inside, battling feelings of helplessness and isolation. I never felt accepted as a child by my family or anyone else.

The only way I could ever fulfill God's promise to prosper me was to find faith. I had to lean on the absolute assurance that He would do exactly what He said He would do. However, for me, the thought of stepping out into unfamiliar territory was terrifying. Fear paralyzed me. As a result, it took me some time to move.

I hated what God had prepared for me. Fear gripped me. Yet, I thank God that He led my husband to me, and I did not allow fear to keep me from experiencing true love.

I am married to a wonderful, God-fearing, oil-slanging, praying man. He has some of the most amazing qualities I have ever seen, as evidenced by his staying with me all these years. I made his life a living hell for fifteen of our twenty-four years of marriage. I took all my fears, baggage, junk, and messed up ways out on him. I wanted someone to pay for the damage my parents had caused. Somebody had to pay, so why not him? Despite this, my husband maintained his love for me, and stood flat-footed in place until I finally woke up.

It took fifteen years for me to realize that I was worthy, and I deserved the love that he was displaying toward me. I was jacked up. If God had not stepped in right on time, my marriage would be over.

I remember feeling like a ton of bricks had been dropped on me as I sat that day in the living room. I replayed the years we shared. God quickly revealed to me all the mistakes I had made and my skewed vision. I had spent fifteen years crying out to the Lord to change my husband when I was the one who needed to be healed and delivered! I felt so numb and embarrassed because he had always been the same. He prayed without ceasing. He studied, and most of all, he loved me. I was the total opposite. I would pray and study, but my level of dedication was nothing like his. At that very moment, I realized he deserved better. I committed to spending the rest of our years together fulfilling my duty as a wife and a woman of God. I am in awe at how the Lord gave him peace and shielded him from all my insecurities, abandonment, and rejection. God shielded him from the baggage I brought into our relationship.

I am overwhelmed by God's love toward me. I am forever grateful that He created me for my husband. Most of all, I am most grateful that He used my husband to love me through and beyond my pain. April 20 of 1996 was one of the greatest days of my life. The second greatest day of my life was March 12, 2010, when I looked my husband in the face to say, "I am sorry." My marriage was now official. I could spend the rest of my life growing with my soul mate. This was yet another testimony of the goodness of Jehovah! God breathed life back into my marriage. For that, I will forever be grateful. This was my first real experience with receiving true love from a man. This was also the day that God kissed me on my forehead and reminded me that I was chosen and forgiven. I was free to live life the way God wanted me to. I was no longer living in the shadows of my parents. The Son had made me whole.

The Bible tells us in Revelation 12:11, *"We overcome by the blood of the lamb and the Word of our testimony."* As I went through the deliverance process, God freed my mind first. Then, He released me from myself and others. I was even on the path of learning to receive love. It was time for the inner healing to begin. I needed to be released to love *me*. All my life, I felt insignificant, like I didn't fit in. Although people were drawn to me and honored my gifts, I still didn't fit. I spent most of my life hiding in the shadows due to fear of my past because I did not love and value myself. How could I? I really did not know how to do that, especially since the persons responsible for my existence never showed me how. This step in the deliverance process was the most pivotal in my journey. I not only learned to love myself, I was re-introduced to a loving God.

In the beginning of this path to healing, I did not quite understand the significance of the Father's love because I didn't have a good example from my earthly father. Since I could not receive love from my biological father, I had trouble receiving love from my heavenly Father. It was in God's Word that He revealed His character to me. I discovered an endless love, which reshaped how I saw myself. God is love, and He tells us to love others as we love ourselves. Yes, loving myself was a requirement for loving others. How could I effectively love others if I did not love myself? Hence, I was led to look up every Scripture on love. This was when my self-love path began. I was used to looking at myself through tainted lenses. But now, I could see (by way of the Holy Spirit) clearly that I was significant and that I mattered to God. I was well on my way to living a life of being healthy, happy, and whole. I was living a good, God-ordained life. Right? Then why was it that just a few months later, instead of sitting in the middle of my living room floor crying, I was lying in a hospital bed, heavily sedated and listening to what sounded like crying?

Out of habit, I reached down. That is when I realized the unimaginable. Tears started to flow. Looking through the tainted lenses of a poverty mindset robs us from living an enjoyable life. However, there some steps we can take to assist us with changing how we see things, such as affirmations. Affirmations help affirm who we are and remind us to keep going. These gentle reminders can be written on paper and placed in restrooms, bedrooms, vehicles, or places of employment. Next, create a "mason jar escape." This involves filling a mason jar with small note cards listing your accomplishments, most enjoyable moments, poems, or scriptures that you can pull from at any time. Using this tool will remind us of the good things that have occurred in our lives. During this process of changing how we "see things," it is vital that we give ourselves some *grace*.

To achieve this, we need to invest in ourselves by getting an accountability partner. Surrounding ourselves with individuals who provide consistency and are not afraid to challenge negative thoughts is key to healing. Reaching out to a Licensed Mental Health Therapist is also helpful in reshaping

THAT NOTHING WILL BE LOST

our thoughts and behaviors. Therapists provide day-to-day tools and coping strategies to assist participants with living a fulfilled life. Finally, we need to give ourselves permission to enjoy life and be happy.

About
Dr. Teresa Moore

Born to a crack-addicted mother, poverty for Dr. Teresa Moore wasn't a *place*, it was a *mindset*. While she naturally grew in stature and age, Teresa's emotional and mental capacity was limited to that of a child strung out on drugs—until she learned to surrender to God. From a life of merely surviving to unapologetically thriving, Dr. Moore soon discovered that to find her true identity, she had to lose sight of self.

Once she tapped into her inner "God-fidence" and redefined what real love looked like, she committed to unlocking others along her journey—reminding them that how you begin does not determine how you finish. In her debut book, *Awakened to Win: 30 Affirmations to Jumpstart Your Day*, Dr. Teresa reminds readers worldwide that everyone was created on purpose, with divine purpose—they simply need to tap into the greatness within. In addition, she serves as a faithful board member of The Fountain for Women, Ruth and Naomi Ministries and Pray Like a Submitted Wife, these are the three candid platforms where women gather to be strengthened and encouraged through the Word of God.

dr.teresamoore@gmail.com

IN MY DAD'S PRESENCE

FELICIA HOLLIS

At the early age of 22, I lost my best friend, my mom. I was divorced and had moved back home with her, still a girl trying to grow up. Mom's death was unexpected and a complete shock for me. I continued with my next best friend, my dad. Some years later, at the age of 27, I now lost my dad unexpectedly. Now, I have lost two parents and my best friends, but I was still trying to grow up. Now a mother myself, being all alone, my children needed a mom who would suddenly grow up. It seemed impossible, not having anyone to help teach me how to pursue growing up. With whom should I engage on this path? Years passed, and there was no one I trusted enough to engage within my growing up process.

My children are now growing up themselves. I supported them the only way I knew how as a single mother, giving them all the love within me that I learned over the years. I leaned on the only person I felt I could trust, my Heavenly Father, all while stumbling in and out of different churches. Still not mature enough for me, until at last, I allowed my trust in my Heavenly Father to place me in the Body of Christ where he knew I could and would finally grow up. We say: What is growing up? Why is growing up necessary? How do we grow in this thing called life as defined by society that we are supposed to grow toward, or be alive at full status to increase by natural development?

Why is it necessary?
So that hopefully and prayerfully, we make the right decisions concerning all areas of our lives. Then, when a parent assists their children in the right direction and decisions, while I was not feeling I was grown up enough, this continually held me at bay mentally, spiritually, and psychologically.

How do you grow up?
Being a grown-up is not so much an age as it is an attitude. It is a stage called maturity, where you develop smart goals, humbleness, taking responsibility for your actions, practicing emotional maturity, and thinking through your decisions. For me, the process of growing up was the most loving and endearing experience I ever endured. My Heavenly Father led me to my part of the body; The River Auburn Hills, where I received a spiritual awakening entitled Sozo. In this deliverance celebration that was led by three ministers, an awakening came.

Sozo was a total transformation for me. On that day, after completing the Sozo questionnaire, I was asked to start praying for any and all things that concerned me. I remember Minister L. asking a question: "What do you see?"
My response: "I see GOD, he is holding a baby in his hands."
   Another question: "Do you recognize the baby?"
   Another response: "Yes! It's me!"

Crying now as my Daddy says to me, "I'm here for you, I love you, Felicia," as he was standing in the most beautiful light I have ever seen. After that three-hour deliverance experience in regular increments, he became *"My Daddy."* He was not just God to me anymore. God was always there with me; I just was not ready to grow up. Sozo took place when I was 72 years old. As I continued growing, I would see him, my Father, holding my hands and pouring into me as time passed. I saw him walking beside me, allowing me to walk without him holding my hand between infancy and a maturing child until finally becoming a young lady, 72 to 74 years old.

Now fully grown up at 76 years, I am no longer missing my Paternal father because I now recognize and realize my spiritual Daddy, who has been with me my entire life. Now don't think I've stopped growing, and I'm enjoying every experience, even when it's spanking time.

For I know He's my Dad, who gives us good things.

I am a senior now, 76 years old, and still making mistakes.
I'll share my last one to let you know how great He is. At seventy-four, I met a gentleman that I got involved with and allowed myself to love him. It was another air of stagnation where I needed more growing up. I had to start psychological therapy all over again by way of Minister L. of the Sozo group. Minister L. was, for all general purposes, my therapist.
As addicts say, "I'm clean now," but it was still a process.

Growing up is a continual process that allows us to come together as sisters of senior hood. Most of us are not aware of or are interested in helping each other. So again, I depended on my Heavenly Father. He gave me wise instructions on how to move to another stage of growth, which prepared me to share my chapter with you wonderful ladies. How can we grow if we have never been taught? At 55, 65, 75, 85 years old, we are very much viable and valuable. We are not a forgotten group, and we will not allow it. Let us grow together. Come with me, side by side. I am reaching out to you. We need to be taught how to prepare to move into senior hood and how to survive it. We were taught how to make it through financially, but not socially, emotionally, intimately, psychologically, or spiritually.

I humbly thank you for comforting me more by reading my chapter. I am just a phone call away. Blessed Be at Peace.

About
Felicia Hollis

I am currently a senior citizen who is now starting to help other senior ladies through consultation. My goal is to start a help ministry for ladies who have been, and are overlooked because we are a misunderstood group. Felecia is a Certified Holistic Therapist, Mom, Grandma and Great Grandma.

(313) 728-6647 | tfme2@aol.com

GRATITUDE

I am so amazed at how God does things. I started out writing a book for myself, and in the middle of writing the book, the inspiration to invite other women to tell their stories as an anthology became a reality. I am so thrilled that I did. As you read this anthology there will be something said by each of these women as they were _"Gathering the Fragments...that nothing will be lost"_ will resonate with you.

Each of these ladies were brave enough to allow you to peek into their personal lives and personal situations, sharing their deepest secrets that will change many lives.

"Gathering the Fragments....that nothing will be lost" taken from the scripture St. John 6:12, "The Feeding of the Five Thousand." It was also an opportunity to use their stories as a means to feed other women with the hope that transformation will take place through reading the process of things they went through.

Through that process, nothing would be lost because of the shame, hurt, guilt, or condemnation they experienced. Now they have emerged whole, healed, and delivered.

I want to compliment and thank each of these women for taking the time to join me without reservations, and in the process, a sisterhood was formed. We cannot negate the power of collaboration, which is so visible in this anthology. I pray each chapter in this book will bless your life and cause lasting change.

I want to encourage you. You have a story. Own your story! Tell your story that nothing will be lost!

Thank you; Tanya Bankston, Karen Cheathem, Lakina Faulks, Barbra Gentry-Pugh, Cathy Hendrix, Prophetess Joyce Hogan, Felicia Hollis, Haydee Irving, Kenya Johnson, Meskerem (Meski) Mekasha, Dr. Teresa Moore, Tanyia Mosley, Tiffany Patton, Beth Weber, Sarah Williams.

You are 15 beautiful women, this is just the beginning.
Go and change the world!
Linda Hunt, Anthology Doctor

Thanks for reading! Please add a short review on Amazon and let us know what you think!

CPSIA information can be obtained
at www.ICGtesting.com
Printed in the USA
JSHW040151151220
10249JS00002B/3